HOW TO BE A MERRY WIDOW

MERRY WIDOW

Life after death for the older lady

Mary Essinger

How to be a Merry Widow

Published by The Conrad Press in the United Kingdom 2018
First published by the Third Age Press 2007

Tel: +44(0)1227 472 874
www.theconradpress.com
info@theconradpress.com

ISBN 978-1-911546-34-4

Typesetting and Cover Design by:
Charlotte Mouncey, www.bookstyle.co.uk

The Conrad Press logo was designed by Maria Priestley.

Printed and bound in Great Britain
by Clays Ltd, Elcograf S.p.A.

By the same author

Mary, Quite Contrary - a memoir

(The Conrad Press 2016)

If ever two were one, then surely we.
If ever man were lov'd by wife, then thee;
If ever wife were happy in a man,
Compare with me ye women if you can.

I prize thy love more than whole mines of gold,
Or all the riches that the east doth hold…

From *To My Dear And Loving Husband*
Anne Bradstreet 16th century

Introduction

This book originated in a short article of the same title I wrote for the British newspaper *The Guardian*.

How to be a Merry Widow shows how a woman can create an interesting life for herself in her new role as a widow.

In this age of splintered families there will be fewer long marriages, and golden weddings may one day come to be regarded as rather quaint.

Those of us who have enjoyed a good marriage are well-placed to enjoy widowhood. It's not that being a widow is so dreadful. It's that being in a companionable marriage is so wonderful. People die but love does not die, we carry it with us.

I wrote most of this in my first year of living alone. Although there have been times when I would have given the rest of life for five minutes in his arms, there is a positive side to being single again and losing a husband sometimes means finding oneself.

Mary Essinger June 2018

Contents

Introduction 7

1. FAREWELL LONELINESS 11

2. HELLO FRIENDS 22

3. DEFENDING YOUR STATUS 30

4. COUPLES, ROMANCE AND SEX 37

5. THE MEANING OF LOSS 46

6. KEEPING WELL, KEEPING HAPPY 52

7. FEELING SAFE 58

8. GO FOR COMEDY GO FOR CULTURE 65

9. SOLO HOUSEKEEPING 75

10. FOOD GLORIOUS FOOD 83

11. GOING PLACES 90

12. SOMEONE FOR THE WEEKEND MADAM? 106

13. MOVING ON 110

Acknowledgements 119

ON THE PHONE TO THE TAXMAN

ME   'Won't I get the married couple's allowance any more?'

TM   'When did he pass?'

ME   'What do you mean?'

TM   'When did he pass away?'

ME   'He died in August.'

TM   'After this tax year ends you will no longer get that allowance.'

ME   'That's terrible. I'd better find a new husband.'

TM   (Polite giggle) 'I don't know about that.'

ME   'Are you married?'

TM   (More giggles) 'Yes, unfortunately I am.'

ME   'What a pity.'

1.

FAREWELL LONELINESS

You are like an animal cut off from the herd; people are social beings and need to be with others. The very word 'solitary' brings fear even to the most hardened criminal. Familiar rooms looked alien to me and a painting we had bought together seemed to stare accusingly. The silent house was eerie and evenings alone were alarming to the point of panic. With desperation as my only companion, all sorts of ideas came to mind: offering a home to a relative, taking in a student, finding a friend to share the house or selling up and moving into a hotel. Anything to prevent living alone. Displayed on the sideboard and windowsills were over one hundred sympathy cards, lovingly chosen, I am sure, and with kind messages. How wonderful it would have been if just one of the senders had phoned to say, 'Can I come round tonight?' I resolved never to send a sympathy card to anyone. Instead I will telephone or write a letter.

Many women of our generation have never lived alone; we left our father's house to move in with our husbands. Being on our own in a house is a complete change in our way of life. Even to watch people passing by makes us feel less isolated.

What can a widow do? First, know that the strangeness of loneliness is merely temporary and soon disappears. Avoid reading anything about bereavement and the various stages of grief; every person is different. Instead, think of widows you know who are leading happy and interesting lives; focus on one you admire, be inspired by her and see what you can learn from the way she tackles life. If she can do it you can do it. Persuade yourself that you are the kind of person who can rise above your present unhappy state.

Plus est en vous. (There is more within you.)

Motto of Gordonstoun School

Look on the positive side, no shirts to iron for a start. Rejoice in your independence. You can do exactly as you like; paint the house pink, invite your chain-smoking brother to stay or relocate to anywhere on the planet. Consider the good things about being alone. For the first time in your life you are free. Spoil yourself; spend his money on chocolate and taxis. You're worth it.

A widower speaks - *Don't get me wrong, I'd a hundred times prefer she was still with me but I do enjoy the freedom.*

Remove yourself from the place of loneliness, your home. Plan at least one social event every day and plan outings to look forward to. Unless you are dying, staying in all day is a bad idea and will make you morose. You may have demanding things to do in the home but go out at least for some part of the day. Too cold? Wear three coats but go out. Raining? Big umbrella but go out. Not feeling too good? Try fresh air and a walk. Fight any temptation to hide away feeling sorry for yourself.

A widow speaks - *I pushed myself with all I had to do, all the paperwork and the flat feeling when it was finished. I'm all right when I'm busy.*

Do not dismiss the idea of going out to work again especially if you are in good health. New legislation is in place preventing discrimination against older people. Study the Situations Vacant columns in newspapers and the cards in job centres; you will be surprised at the variety of work listed. One friend invigilates exams in a college and another is a life model for an art class.

Plan a personal project; something to occupy your thoughts and energy; something to get your teeth into. Perhaps a re-design of the garden or a spare room. Family history is absorbing and so is academic study, especially if there is a certificate at the end as a target. Open University courses are hugely life-enhancing and there will be many students older than you, unless you're a hundred and two. Busy people are not lonely. A friend tells me that widows are in a trance for the first year; perhaps I'm in a trance writing this.

A widow speaks - *I play the piano when I'm fed up. Sometimes I have to force myself but it makes such a difference. The music takes me away.*

Have a daily paper delivered. You don't have to read it all and recycling is a nuisance but a national paper keeps you in touch with the world. You'll probably be waking early anyway and a cheering routine is to make a cup of

13

tea, collect the paper, return to your bedroom and do the crossword or that exasperating sudoku.

A friend tells me a dog is not only wonderful company but everybody else with a dog will stop for a chat with you; she says dogs make people happy. I'm toying with the idea of a cat.

A widow speaks - *If you're on your own I don't think you could live without a dog. Who would you talk to? When I go home he greets me as if I've been away for a year.*

Take risks; go to a show alone. You will be sitting in a row of people at the theatre just as you would with a husband. You can walk in a busy park alone saying hello to children.

Some activities are even better on your own, shopping and libraries for example, where you can browse forever. But going to parties by yourself is definitely not advisable. It is one thing to stand with a drink in your hand making small talk knowing there's a husband in the corner grumbling and wanting to go home and quite another matter if he is not there. You feel lost. Invited to parties, merry widows should ask if they can bring a friend.

A widow speaks - *The worse thing was coming home after an evening out and having no-one to talk to about it.*

Merry widows stride into the best hotels as if they own the place, knowing that afternoon tea in a top hotel costs no more than a café and that they'll find a better class of customer there. Carry a book to give an air of independence and if you see somebody who looks interesting, smile and get into conversation. Merry widows enjoy talking to strangers; a chat with a stranger can bring much interest to the day. Risk a snub and do not assume that young people only like talking to other young people. You are at an age when conversation becomes easy.

Be open to adventure; boldness has magic in it. Do things you could not do as a couple. My young decorator was painting the kitchen ceiling and I didn't know what to do about cooking a meal. On the spur of the moment I asked him if he fancied going out for lunch at the local pub. 'Oh, yes,' he said, 'but I haven't brought any money.' I told him I was paying but we were going in his van. He sat eating lunch in his painting clothes like a proper workman and it was a really enjoyable break in a dull day. How's that for freedom? You can't do that if you're married and you can't do that if you're young, but you can do it if you're a merry widow.

On a day visit to another town I called in a shop for a leisurely manicure; see, you can't do that with a husband, can you?

Before long I was chatting with a young girl from Vietnam doing a terrific job on my neglected fingers. Her language was limited and she thanked me for the conversation, saying she was shy and preferred writing English to speaking it.

After a while you will find that if you've been somewhere interesting with other people in the daytime you will actually look forward to being at home on your own in the evening; you really will, especially if you rearrange the furniture to make yourself a cosy sitting-area away from the world's troubles. Keep this space tidy and inviting, with everything you need, such as a phone and reading matter, within easy reach.

A widow speaks - *I was in a fog for the first year but once that was over with all its anniversaries I felt better. I said to myself, 'This is how it will be forever, make the best of it'. I enjoy my life now.*

Now that you are free you could take a fresh look at your family.

Many relatives today are out of touch with each other through divorce or long working hours. Young people do not realise the importance of family until they are older, and as an aunt you could take on some responsibility for helping them to maintain contact with each other, such as by reminding them of a birthday of one of your younger relatives. They really will appreciate your interest. Keep lists of their birthdays adding family news to the cards you send. If they don't send one back to you it doesn't matter at all. Keep records of names of newborns and if you post birthday cards to babies it's not so important to send one to the parents. Occasionally you could invite all the cousins with their children for tea. It may be the only time they see each other and they will love it. Why wait till your funeral?

After the first few weeks, start to bring order into your new life by making a weekly routine for yourself, something for Thursdays, another for Saturdays; routines help to prevent loneliness by giving you something to look forward to. You will need to dress earlier in the mornings now or wear an attractive housecoat because there's nobody there to answer the door for you, and merry widows must look pretty at all times.

A widower speaks - *Since my wife died two months ago I've been overwhelmed with invitations from friends and relatives. My cousin insists I go abroad on holiday with him and his family. I've been taken to football matches and asked home to lots of meals. It's all very nice but there are times when I'd just rather be left alone. Perhaps they think a man can't look after himself without a woman. Still, people tell me that invitations fall off after a while. It's funny how I take notice when people say things like this.*

But there's no getting away from it, you will sometimes feel isolated and lonely, usually when you are tired. At such moments say to yourself the magic words, 'This feeling will pass.' Do something. Hand-sewing is a most pleasant activity, save some mending to do and put Radio 4 on. Listening to the radio and sewing is a splendid way to spend an evening at home; for some reason the radio is better company than television. Remember that married people get fed up sometimes as well. They really do. Millions of people live alone, most of them by choice; thirty percent of newly built houses are for single occupancy, it's a growth area.

Think of widowhood as just another stage of life like getting married or having a first baby.

With good health and good friends you can create an exciting new life for yourself and one of these mornings you'll wake up singing.

Daylight, I must wait for the sunrise.

I must think of a new life
And I mustn't give in.

From the musical *Cats*
by T.S. Eliot and Trevor Nunn

DIARY

A bank holiday is a testing time for a merry widow and here
I am on a Saturday morning. It's far too wet for the rambling
club's seven-mile walk and friends will probably be involved
with their families on a bank holiday. I'm facing the prospect
of a whole day with nothing to do.

Although it's only 8.30am, I've decided to drive to town.
I know a quiet road to park before strolling down a leafy
Victorian walkway into the city. My son has a book called
'Spellbound' coming out today and I'll head for Waterstones
to see it displayed. After that I'll nip into M&S before finding
somewhere for lunch. That's the plan and when I come back
I'll report on its outcome...

Four hours later.

Most things in life happen by chance and on the pavement
where I parked was a sign, 'Show Apartment Now Open.'
What a beautiful lady greeted me, so much make-up so expertly
applied, it must have taken her ages. She had used everything,
blusher, black lines round the eyes, eye shadow on the lids
and brow, foundation and scarlet lipstick with an amazingly
sharp edge. Her fingernails fluttering over the brochure were
long, pink and a perfect almond shape. How does she do it?
She was plump with the clear complexion of a plump lady and

as she tripped ahead to show me an apartment her black lace skirt danced from side to side.

The apartment was delightful, with a balcony. Everything was top quality from the inbuilt dishwasher to the Italian taps and I pictured myself living there.

But the merry widow rule is to be wary of making big decisions for a whole year in case you make decisions you later regret. I still had three months to go.

The walk into the city crosses a park where a tramp, with four Tesco bags, sits on a bench drinking from a can; I smile and wave Good Morning. We singles have to look out for each other.

On the shelf in Oxfam I pick up a book called 'The World's Greatest Letters,' which looked ideal for dipping into at bedtime so that was my first purchase. The second was a disposable camera to take pictures of Waterstones' massive display of my son's book. But there was not a massive display at all; just five copies downstairs in the English language department. Who would go all the way down there to look for it? I carried the five books upstairs and rearranged them on the main display table near the entrance.

By now the town was full of teenagers, with their children in pushchairs under plastic covers. On the way back I passed a young mother singing, 'The wheels on the bus go round and round,' as she followed me up the hill with her pram. Today's babies face forward into the wind and it was sad that the child could not see its mother as she sang.

Thinking it would be a pleasant place to shelter for ten minutes I followed two women into a church. Inside a notice warned that a CCTV camera was in operation, even God gets spied on. I didn't stay.

Further along was the city's art gallery, with its impressive frontage of Doric columns. A smiling young woman at the desk was telling visitors they couldn't leave their wet umbrellas with her.

'Do I have to carry my shopping round as well?' I asked. She said she was sorry, but there was no longer a facility for depositing bags because of insurance. When I asked what her job was she smiled and said she was there to make visitors feel welcome.

The park was now full with the youth of all nations playing football, using sports bags for goalposts. Young children running and laughing excitedly in the rain, such a joy to watch.

Facing me at the top of the hill was the apartment building I was shown that morning. It looked like home.

Later in the day the sun shone and I planted out a dozen busy Lizzies ready for summer.

Afterwards, an evening writing this, grateful for good health, hair that looks its best in damp weather and looking forward to bedtime with 'The World's Greatest Letters.'

FUN THINGS TO DO ALONE

Pack a picnic, pack a book and find a bench in a busy park. Leave a space and soon you'll be joined by people wondering who the interesting lady with the picnic basket and sunhat could be.

Go to town, buy a box of good-quality French soap, go home and take a bath with it.

2.

HELLO FRIENDS

My friends are God's apology for my relations.

Author unknown

Anyone who has lived in the same area for thirty years or more will know many, many people and on a visit to town they will see familiar faces on the street, in shops and in cafes. Some will hardly warrant a glance; others will stop for a chat, 'How well you're looking. The facelift was worth every penny.'

At the next level is the surprise encounter, a fancy-seeing-you moment. 'How was Peru? Your husband was eaten by a jaguar? Oh, what a shame! Never mind, see you on Tuesday.'

You might speak to a relative, 'Did Aunt Sylvia leave you the grand piano? Did Jim get parole?'

Bumping into a close friend is the best surprise. 'Come on, let's go for coffee. Of course there's time.' And in the café there will almost certainly be other people you know.

This amazing friendship network is the merry widow's support system; the prop that holds her up, so think carefully before doing anything silly like moving to Spain.

From this remarkable circle will be those who are special; and what a joy to a merry widow these friends are. Such friendships, and there are usually no more than about six of them, must be nurtured by regular meetings, chatting on the phone and never making demands. Hang a Year Planner chart on the wall with their birthdays, mine's behind the lavatory door. Keep a stock of cards ready to send.

A man must keep his friendships in good repair.

Samuel Johnson

The balance of feeling between close friends is fragile and easily damaged by a careless remark or action. Older women are usually extremely nice to each other and rarely fall out but when they do it is a disaster. Make it up immediately. I fell out with a friend and my instinct was to have nothing more to do with her. But I'd known this person for over thirty years and could not afford to lose her. I waited a week then rang to ask her out for lunch. She came; neither of us mentioned the falling out. Friendship is instinctive with women and they will rally round a new widow. Friends keep us balanced; to say someone has no friends indicates that something is not right.

I have lost friends. Some through death; and others through a sheer inability to cross the street.

Virginia Woolf

With your new freedom you can invite people whenever you like. Don't wait for others to ask you, they might think you'd rather be alone. Risk a refusal. A cup of tea on a Sunday afternoon is one idea; lots of singles are at a loose end on Sundays. Ask three or four, you don't need to entertain them; they'll never stop talking. Women love to talk. Some call it gossip, others call it keeping up with vital snippets of news. Plan an evening at home where you watch a film with three or four others. Offer a glass of sherry when they come, ask if they are all comfortable and switch on. Half way through, stop the film and serve coffee or tea, at which point you can all decide whether to carry on watching or not.

Someone who can be relied on always to say yes when you suggest an outing is extremely valuable. She may not be the world's most exciting companion but grab her.

Friendships depend on tolerance and one of the compensations of getting old, and there are many, is that we become more tolerant of the strange ways of others.

'Lord, make me tolerant of my friends in the eternal hope they will tolerate me.'

Now you're on your own you will need to make new single friends because foursomes will not work any more. In any case it's good to cultivate people who have not known you as part of a couple. Surprisingly, older women make friends easily and you will need a notebook, not bits of paper, for the names and numbers of all your new acquaintances.

To widen your circle be self-motivating. Take up joinery. Become a Scrabble expert. Pick up leaflets at the library, read notices in local newspapers and shop windows. Talk to people. Ask them about the organisations they belong to; you'll be amazed how many clubs and societies will welcome you. Try them all out for a week or two before paying up as a member. Rambling clubs are particularly good for making new contacts because it's easy to talk while you are walking along. I was out this morning in a group of fifteen; they were talking about finding a good plumber, where to buy the best turkeys and what to do with a surplus sideboard. How about that for networking? If you join any group you may feel a bit sidelined the first time; don't expect everybody to make a fuss of you, they want to talk to their friends. Make allowances, and, if it's the other way round and a newcomer joins your group, make sure you are the first to speak to them.

U3A stands for University of the Third Age. It's not a university and I don't know what the Third Age is. But it's a brilliant movement and groups are springing up everywhere. The idea is that retired people get together to share their skills and knowledge with others. This might be such topics as bird watching, art, bell ringing or literature; the list depends upon members who are willing to set up a group. Once a month there's a meeting with a speaker and a chance to find out about the different activities. Most U3As have a lunch club and a travel group. Since joining a local U3A I have been to Switzerland, Barcelona and Venice. Use a page-a-day diary for the details of your exciting activities, together with a brief note on your kitchen wall calendar; if you trust your memory for dates and times it will let you down.

Team up with happy people because happiness is catching. If someone is basically unhappy there's not much you can do about it so leave them alone. My father told me some people are only happy when they're miserable.

Learn something new. Bridge for example. This is a marvellous game which you can play till you're a hundred. Like many worthwhile things it takes a little learning, you can't pick it up as you go along. Find a beginners' class at a community centre or even the U3A. Once you've mastered the general rules you learn by playing. You can play at home or at a bridge club. Bridge clubs are full of widows all having a great time together.

Bridge friendships last for years because the game doesn't depend on physical fitness and players move heaven and earth to get to the card table especially if there are bidding boxes for the hard of hearing and cards with big numbers for the hard of seeing.

A softly, softly approach is needed with a person you would like to go out with for an evening but do not know very well. Nothing puts others off like appearing pushy or needy but on the other hand if you wait for others to ask you it may not happen at all.

Suppose you have cleverly collected a file of information on events such as bus trips, theatres and exhibitions. Try a casual phone call, 'I'm looking for somebody to go to the theatre with next Friday, I don't suppose you are free?'

The phrase, 'I'm looking for somebody,' suggests there are others to ask and you won't be stuck if she can't come.

On another occasion you could say, 'Will you let me know if you can come on a trip to London on July the twenty-first?' The words, 'Let me know' give people time to think; the phone is often too quick for making decisions. If you are invited out and can't go be sure to say, 'Please ask me again I would really enjoy your company.'

Be prepared in case someone is unwise enough to say to you, 'What are you doing next Tuesday?' If your answer is 'nothing' you could find yourself agreeing to something dreadful like a fancy dress barbecue. Say you are not sure or you have a hairdressing appointment. If the invitation is a free ticket to the ballet say you'll change the appointment.

After a party where somebody has gone to a lot of trouble it is never enough to say, 'thank you' as you leave because this is a mere formality and means nothing. Ring the following morning when she will be full of doubts about how well the evening went. 'I just wanted to say how much I enjoyed last night, it was wonderful.' Mention something in detail, 'The fifteen-year-old conjurer was terrific, thanks again.' She will love you forever and invite you every time. A really big do like a wedding requires, of course, a letter of thanks.

Be scrupulous with money matters and pay your way. It's better to pay too much than to be thought mean. On a long journey to a ramble I might ask one of the men for a lift; men seem to like driving more than women. I buy the driver a drink, pay car-park charges or hand over a little money, 'Please put this in your grandchild's money box.' No refusals so far.

If a friend books tickets for a show, pay her immediately or write it in your diary in case you forget. At the end of an evening out say, 'Are we both straight with money matters?' If she says she'll treat you thank her nicely but say you prefer to be independent.

If you've never learned to drive and your husband dies you could be in trouble and become a burden to your friends. I have heard people say, 'It's no good asking so-and-so because you have to collect her and take her back.' The cost and inconvenience of driving you about is not the main problem; it is the responsibility. What can you do? Investigate public transport; there are more trains and buses than you think. Consider moving to live on a bus route. If you don't run a car you're saving money; work out what the weekly saving is, put it in a pot and take a good look at it. This is price of your independence. Spend it on taxis; use the same company each time and they'll get to know you.

When you're with friends you don't talk about your husband do you? And certainly not about things that you did together years ago. Nobody wants to listen. You *know* he was the cleverest and most perfect man ever. Why boast?

The great Roman Emperor, Augustus, became angry when people commiserated with him for having no grandchildren. He said it was wrong to criticise the gods. Talking about grandchildren is not an interesting topic and the cute things they say don't sound at all cute when repeated to those who do not know them. There may be people listening who have no grandchildren, me for instance. You need daughters for grandchildren; sons clear off to the other end of the planet. You need six daughters and don't let them go to university because if you do they'll want to be presidents of engineering companies and wear men's suits and have their first baby when they are about fifty years old. I'm sure grandchildren bring great joy, but don't talk about them all the time. It's embarrassing.

When you think about it, much of social life involves avoiding embarrassment. The gift your friends bring you is smaller than yours, embarrassment. You made a simple meal; they bring expensive flowers; she came too early, you were not dressed – all embarrassment. But it's part of the friendship game and it's through friends that merry widows create for themselves an exciting new life.

Mother, 'Grandma's gone to heaven.'
Small child, 'I bet that's not all it's cracked up to be.'

3.

DEFENDING YOUR STATUS

And there came a certain poor widow and she threw in two mites.

St Mark

Families naturally prefer widows to unmarried mothers. But only just.

Jean-Paul Sartre

You will notice these quotations present a picture of a pathetic woman of low status in society. Although that was long before the NHS and terrific moisture creams, things have not changed that much today. Widows are low in the pecking order. Men have status, couples have status, married women and young women have status but not elderly widows. When I turned up with a friend at the pub where I used to go regularly with my husband we were given, instead of the usual table, a much smaller one. When I protested I was told the bigger tables were reserved for groups of three; I couldn't help noticing that some were occupied by couples.

If you are standing at the bar and the man behind gets served first, smile sweetly and say, 'Excuse me, I think I'm before you.' I once asked a barman why men were served first and he said it was assumed the woman was with the man and suggested that to get attention women should hold out the money in the way men do.

On a weekend away, in the middle of the night, I got out of bed to check the curtain. I rarely lock hotel doors in case of fire and at that precise moment it opened and from the light of the hallway I saw a man entering. Yelling loudly I rushed forward and pushed him back. 'I'm so sorry, I'm so sorry,' he kept repeating in a confused and feeble way. His wife came out of their next-door room and apologized for him. Next morning I soon stopped telling friends about my experience because all of them, women and men, made jokes about it on the lines of, 'Did you ask him to stay for breakfast?' or 'Did you lock him in?' They would not have dreamed of making jokes if I had been with my husband, or if I was a young woman alone.

Be aware of your low status and do something about it. If you can afford a nice car, don't drive round in a small ancient one; a car gives a merry widow importance in the community, it's OK to be young driving a shabby car but not if you are reasonably old. If you can afford a good seat at a show book it instead of a cheap one. If you can afford a taxi don't wait around for buses in the cold. For personal status dress nicely in the house and when you come home from an outing keep your smart clothes on, it feels good and improves your mood. You are a merry widow. You have freedom and independence. Let it show.

A widow speaks - *When you're a widow you have to speak up for yourself because there's nobody there to do it for you.*

Sometimes men say things to me they would not dream of saying if I was with my husband. A man at Badminton said I was putting on weight. You can't let people get away with saying things like that to you. I told him he was an ugly pig.

Be assertive with workmen in your house, if they come late be firm, 'I expected you earlier,' and there's no need for strangers to know you live alone, let them assume there's a man in the house, put his hat on display. If you're asked where your husband is say he's out. Be business-like and avoid chatting. If you must offer cups of tea, and you don't have to, wait till they've finished the job or done at least an hour's work. Do not allow liberties, they cannot use your toilet without your permission; they wouldn't do it if your husband was present. You're the boss now; behave like one. After a series of phone calls from the carpet fitter saying he would be delayed I said, 'My husband wants me to cancel the whole thing.' He came immediately.

A widow told me that a few weeks after her husband died their decorator called to give an estimate for some work. She said he began touching her all over and she was very frightened. When I asked why she didn't get angry and show him the door she said she had no confidence at the time and felt vulnerable. In the end he left when she started to cry. Another friend said her late husband's golfing friend came to visit, followed her into the kitchen and put his arms round her saying he'd always fancied her. 'Why didn't you go for him with a rolling pin?' I asked. She said she was too scared and the next time he came, instead of answering the door, she hid behind a curtain.

It is hard to believe that some women are so meek. A man might misinterpret such diffidence as encouragement. Probably it is a generation difference; most of today's young women would not allow such appalling behaviour from men.

For a real assessment of how some human societies regard widows consider this. In parts of India the practice of suttee, where widows were put on the funeral pyres of their dead husbands, survived until the 1920s.

> *The fact is that age is respectable just as long as it asserts itself, maintains its proper rights and is not enslaved to anyone.*

> Cicero (65 BC)

Don't let others talk you into doing things you don't want to do. If you want a happy life you have to be a bit selfish. Our time is precious and limited. Running a home, developing a rewarding social life and recovering from loss will fill your days. Any spare time is for having a hairdo or messing about with plants, it is not for the convenience of others.

We are programmed from girlhood to be friendly to everybody, to smile sweetly all the time and never answer back. We say Yes when we mean No.

Boys are brought up differently. When a man says, 'I've got to help my brother-in-law paint his shed on Saturday,' he means he wants to do it and he's looking forward to having a great time.

When a woman says. 'I've got to organise a fund-raising stall on Saturday,' she doesn't want to do it at all, but she has to because

- nobody else offered
- she can't let the group down
- she didn't know how to say 'no'.

Today's young people work long hours and have little time for the hobbies and interests older people enjoyed when they were young. As a result there is serious shortage of volunteers for the committees of various groups and older people are in great demand. Once anyone resigns from a committee it is extremely difficult to find a replacement and long established societies all over the country have had to disband. If you are asked to help out, and only if you really want to, say you will do it for a year and see this is written in the minutes. If you are already embroiled in some time-consuming activity, losing a husband might be a good time to give your notice in. How can you be a merry widow if you tie yourself down with jobs that others think would be good for you? I have heard people say this kind of thing:

'Let's ask so and so to deliver leaflets round, she's lost her husband, she'll be glad of something to do. Take her mind off it.'

Here's how to refuse:

Look in the mirror, place the tip of your tongue behind the upper teeth, push the lips forward then release the tongue and say NO. Practise it. If this is too difficult try saying, 'Nobody' then stop before you come to 'body.' You're trying it now aren't you? I can see you.

If you don't want to do something, smile and say, 'No, I don't fancy that.' You do not have to give a reason and don't make excuses because excuses can be argued against; there's no argument against not fancying something.

A widow speaks - *I look after a grandchild twice a week while my daughter goes to work. It was easy when there were two of us but I get that tired at the end of the day and I don't know how to tell her.*

A widow speaks - *I wish I didn't have to make the teas for the AGM, I'm over eighty and worry about it.*

Women have an instinct for putting something back into society and charitable work of your own choosing is quite a different matter as long as it does not mean mixing with unhappy people in depressing surroundings. Major charities, such as Save the Children, have local branches that organise fund-raising events. Becoming involved with these activities can be fulfilling and an excellent way to meet interesting people and broaden your social life. As a way in you could start by going to one of their events, but keep your status by doing only what you want to do and only what brings you pleasure. Learn to say No.

Does that sound selfish? Yes, but believe me it will make you happier.

FUN THINGS TO DO ALONE

- Create moves to an Abba record

- Paint a door

- Teach yourself to juggle.

Surprised by Joy

Surprised by joy - impatient as the wind -
I turn'd to share the transport - O with whom
But Thee - deep buried in the silent tomb,
That spot which no vicissitude can find?

Love, faithful love recall'd thee to my mind -
But how could I forget thee? Through what power
Even for the least division of an hour
Have I been so beguiled as to be blind

To my grievous loss? That thought's return
Was the worst pang that sorrow ever bore
Save one, one only when I stood forlorn,
Knowing my heart's best treasure was no more.
That neither recent time nor years unborn
Could to my sight thy heavenly face restore.

William Wordsworth

4.
COUPLES, ROMANCE AND SEX

Before long, merry widows begin to notice the world is full of couples, queuing at Sainsbury's bakery, on beaches throwing frisbies and sitting at every damn table in every damn restaurant. Couples, everywhere you go and the pang of envy when you see them is troubling. Of course they're not all getting on well together and sometimes they're arguing, or they are sullen and silent, but they're together and that's what matters.

A wife at the bridge club seems to look forward to her husband making mistakes in order to tell him off in front of others.

'You silly man, you must bid the hearts first,' she snaps.

How I wish I had the courage to say, 'Leave him alone and be glad you've got him.' One of these days I'll say it, but to tell the truth I'm a bit frightened of her myself. No husband is perfect of course and there were times when I told mine he didn't deserve a wife like me, but I have no reason to feel any remorse as we shared a great love.

A widow speaks - *Sometimes if I stop and talk to married people I notice the wife will drag him away. It's very strange. The older a wife gets the more she needs a husband as a carer. Some women are frightened of widows.*

A widow speaks - *I went on a walking holiday and found I was the only single person among five couples. It was awful. The organiser did what she could to make me welcome but all week I felt like a spare part. Tables in the dining rooms were set for four and one morning when I sat at one, this horrible woman snapped at me, 'This is OUR table.'*

A couple you've known for a long time might invite you home for a meal and you could occasionally invite them back but if they ask you to go out somewhere with them think carefully.

If you suspect one of them has talked the other into it you must make an excuse and refuse because you'll feel uncomfortable.

Some married couples would be delighted with the sparkling company of a merry widow, but do you really want to be the evening's entertainment? Ask yourself what's in it for you. They go home afterwards and you are on your own. Think about it. I was invited to the theatre by one couple but they were much younger and I was a sort of mother for the evening and enjoyed that.

If you do accept an invitation let the man make any decisions.

We know about these things, don't we girls?

A widow speaks - *My husband and I were friends for years with the couple across the road. The four of used to go on holiday together and for days out. From the moment my husband died she did not speak to me again and she would cross the street to avoid me. I was heartbroken because I regarded her as my best friend. After a week or two I went into her garden and said, 'Excuse me but have I done something wrong?' She said,*

'It's just one of those things,' and carried on weeding. They've moved away now.

A widow speaks - *I sometimes go on holiday with a couple I've known for years and get on well with both of them. But I don't go every time because I would hate them to think they are obliged to invite me.*

At a social gathering the couples, as usual, were sitting with other couples but they couldn't hear each other speak over the riotous laughter coming from the merry widow's table, (especially when we ordered one pudding and six spoons.)

A widow speaks - *When you're a couple you can just say to a husband, 'Let's go out somewhere.' I miss that.*
  Couples who are insensitive enough to display signs of affection to each other in your presence should be boiled in oil very slowly.

> *You cannot call it love, for at your age*
> *The heyday in the blood is tame, it's humble*
> *And waits upon the judgement...*

Hamlet to his mother

There are a lot of men around longing for an affair with a mature widow. Sensitive, intellectual men, who think nothing of spending an hour at the florist assembling the perfect bouquet. Good looking, smart men with a high standard of personal hygiene. Men skilled in the art of romantic seduction, who regard an amorous afternoon as the highest form of pleasure, to be savoured at leisure to the strains of Rachmarinov in a hotel room with a balcony overlooking the sea or by a sylvan stream in spring.

There are probably lots of men like this, only I've never come across one, and merry widows don't waste time looking. Merry widows enjoy the fantasy and go shopping. There are more things in life than sex, cake for instance. At her Ruby Wedding a friend told me they got on much better once they both accepted that the physical side of their marriage was over. But of course that's just her. It might not be you.

A widow speaks - *Women are not so interested in sex. We crave love and affection but not sex. The papers and TV are on about it all the time and we're made to feel there's something wrong with us if we have no interest. I had a man friend once and we got on well together but when it came to the crunch I just burst into tears; I couldn't do it.*

But of course there are plenty of women who like sex as much as men do, or even more.

A widow speaks - *Of course I miss the sex but I have a nice time with Anne Summers. And don't you dare put that in your book.*

A merry widow flirts. Any good-looking man under forty will do, and let's face it, all men under forty are good-looking and they love a flirtation with an older lady, they know it's in fun.

Merry widows do not flirt with over fifties, it's dangerous, they think you are after them and get frightened.

You weren't expecting to find a new husband were you? There are nowhere near enough to go round.

As a service to my readers and purely in the interest of social research I've been studying the availability of men suitable for merry widows to marry.

Investigations led me to a variety of likely locations, delicatessens, vets' waiting rooms, golf clubs, cross-country events, pub gardens, computer shops and all main line stations to London. Not one suitable candidate.

There was a man in the café at Debenhams, intelligent-looking in a pale grey suit, reading *The Guardian*, and I decided he might do for a new husband. I checked my lipstick, sprinted across to borrow the salt and almost collided with a glamorous young woman - not a uniformed member of Debenham's café staff but obviously his wife - carrying a tray of tea to his table.

Men aged between fourteen and ninety-five are attracted to young women. Ask any man who he fancies most, a glamorous pensioner or the twenty-year-old at Tesco's check out. You know the answer. Men are programmed by nature to go for the fertility of clear complexions and pert bosoms. My aunt Kate once told me that a man showing interest in an older woman was looking for a carer. Run. Run far away. Besides who wants a man who can't carry his own tea tray?

Research on bereavement at Liverpool University found that twice as many men remarry as women. One reason given is that widowers miss the companionship. They tend not to have as many friends as widows; men do not go to concerts together, for example.

Another was the domestic comfort that men need, whereas women welcome the freedom and liberation of living alone.

My view is that a man on his own will have women queuing up at his door.

A widow speaks - *Be sure to tell readers that some men chase widows for their money.*

Settle for being single, people come and go and we're all on our own in one way or another. Many married people wish they were not. Enjoy your single life. Look after yourself and treat yourself well. You're a heroine. You're a merry widow. People will envy your independence.

But if someone comes into your world, and you find yourself adoring them, seize the day. Nobody knows what's round the corner. I was sixty-six when my first novel was published; nice things do happen to older people.

A widow speaks - *I went on holiday with a friend. On the first night as we entered the dining room two men were walking behind us and the waiter assumed the four of us were all together and put us at one table. They were nice men and my friend regularly now spends holidays with one of them.*

Women often make the first move in acquiring a man friend. You could say something like, 'I'm going to a concert with a friend, would you like to come with us?' Try it.

The widows I know who have paired up with a man don't marry them. They go on holiday or spend weekends together but they don't live together. When I asked a widow why she didn't marry her man friend she said she didn't want his dirty shoes on her carpet. When I asked a widower why men preferred to remarry he pointed out that if a man was fond of a woman he would not want to lose her and marriage would bind her to him.

A widow speaks - *It would be difficult if I met somebody now, I've been on my own for ten years and I would have to give up too much.*

A reliable male friend with no romantic complications is extremely useful to a merry widow. If there's somebody you've known for a long time he could be worth cultivating. Here's what to say. 'I'm not after you but if you fancy a game of chess sometime give me a call.'

If he comes don't dress up and don't flirt.

Some occasions are more enjoyable with an escort and for something like a wedding you could ask a male relative to go with you. Or you could be cheeky. 'Next week is the Christmas dinner,' I announced to my writing group, 'I've bought a ticket and a frock and now I'm looking for a bloke to go with. If anybody has a spare granpa I'm interested.' A nice man at the back spoke up, 'I'll go with you.'

A widower speaks - *I was in the supermarket one Saturday afternoon choosing a video and nearby was a young woman. I've always been a bit cheeky and I said, 'I've got my video and a bottle of wine now all I need is somebody like you to*

come round and watch it with me. I expect you're spoken for.'
She said, 'Yes I'm spoken for but my mother's not, she'll come.'
I told her I was only joking and too old at seventy. She said I
wasn't old and her mother would be pleased.

I said, 'Well, here's my phone number, tell her to ring me if
she wants to come.' We've been married a year now.

The novelist Henry Fielding - *When widows exclaim loudly*
against second marriages, I would always lay a wager that the
man, if not the wedding-day, is absolutely fixed on.

FUN THINGS TO DO ALONE

- Take a train ride to another town

- Visit open gardens

- Contact your RSPCA and arrange to take a dog for a
  walk.

Remember me

'Remember me when I am gone away,
Gone far away into the silent land;
When you can no more hold me by the hand,
Nor I half turn to go, yet turning stay.
Remember me when no more day by day
You tell me of our future that you plann'd;
Only remember me; you understand
It will be late to counsel then or pray.
Yet if you should forget me for a while
And afterwards remember, do not grieve:
For if the darkness and corruption leave
A vestige of the thoughts that once I had,
Better by far you should forget and smile
Than that you should remember and be sad.'

Christina Rossetti

5.

THE MEANING OF LOSS

The intimate companionship of marriage is the best thing life has to offer.

Bertrand Russell

To ignore the experience of a husband's death in a book entitled *How to be a Merry Widow* would be entirely wrong, so this section is about loss.

Merry widows deal with loss by first recognising and accepting the enormity of it. Loss is not merely another word for death, loss is far more than that, loss is the life-changing, bewildering, vacuum in the wake of death with its dramatic finality. The empty chair at mealtimes, the empty fireside chair at evening, the vacant passenger seat and the cruel, cold void in the double bed all attest to the complete and total absence of his physical presence.

The dear familiar sounds of the daily routine have been stolen from you. The electric shaver in the morning, the clatter of pots in the kitchen, the lawnmower's rhythmic burr, the calling from room to room, the sweet music of his key in the lock and the snatches of his little songs are gone. Even the arguments that showed you were alive to the differences between each other have been taken from you.

Widows lose the pleasure of giving and receiving affection, the hand that reaches across as you watch a favourite TV programme together; those small intimacies that are the jewels of ordinary days.

No longer will he sit opposite in a restaurant, nor walk with you in a field of lambs. Your holiday companion has gone and social events will never be the same.

Loss is the absence of someone to deal with money matters, happily scribbling away on bits of paper, someone to share a joke, the newspaper and the crossword. All this has gone.

You lose someone to change a plug, hold the stepladder, check the car tyres and deal with a spider. You lose a carer who'll fetch your prescription, rub your back, make the Lemsip and hot water bottle and tell you off for worrying about nothing.

Not everything is lost. People die but love does not die and I feel my beloved husband is still looking after me. The contentment that comes from being cherished and being desired stays with you. And when his apple tree bursts into blossom do not weep because he cannot see it, be grateful for all the years when he could. The life you shared will sustain you; giving strength and confidence to make an interesting new life with its potential for adventure and excitement.

A widow speaks - *To be unhappy would be to throw away everything he gave me.*

A friend speaks - *If you think it's tough being a widow you should try being divorced.*

Be strong for your children. You have lost only a husband; they have lost a father and cannot cope with a mother going to pieces as well. Show them you can be independent and they'll come to see you more often. Each child will react differently to their father's death and there is no way of knowing how it will affect them. My younger son flew back to San Diego with a case full of his dad's clothes and the words, 'I'm not so afraid of death now.' The older one said, 'All I want is in my pocket,' referring to the five-page letter his father wrote to him when he was one week old.

I find a rose from you among my souvenirs.

1930s song.

The French novelist Colette: *It's so curious; one can resist tears and 'behave' well in the hardest hours of grief. But then someone makes you a friendly sign behind a window – or one notices that a flower that was in bud only yesterday has suddenly blossomed, or a letter slips from a drawer - and everything collapses.*

Find one special photograph where he looks happy, perhaps taken in the days of his vigour, have it enlarged, display it mounted in a frame and every time you glance at it your heart will leap with joy.

Here's an interesting thing. A friend who works with confused older people tells me that even women with

Altzheimers disease know when it's their wedding anniversary. They don't know the date but they know it's their anniversary. My friend thinks it could be something to do with the time of the year, the hours of daylight, certain flowers and trees that are in bloom or something about the air.

A stranger stopped me in the street and asked if my husband was all right because she had not seen him for some time. When I told her he'd died she touched my shoulder, as people do, and said she was very sorry, adding, 'I used to see him going shopping. Such a smart man in his cap.' I had never thought of him in this way. Glancing up during a bridge game a friend briefly remarked, 'We all loved him you know.' I was so moved because I did not know. If people only knew the enduring comfort and pleasure of their casual remarks.

A widow speaks - *I find myself doing things I used to nag him about, such as putting forks in the wrong drawer. I feel truly awful about that.*

A widow speaks - *The things I should have said and didn't say, and the things I said and should not have said, really worry me.*

Be warned, memory reminds us not only of what we have lost but of what we did not always appreciate when we had it. But do not be hard on yourself if there were times when you were not as kind as you should have been. You are human. Remember the song 'You always hurt the one you love.' Imagine the situation was reversed; would you want him to be unhappy because he was sometimes not kind to you? He loved you and you loved him. That's all that matters.

FUN THINGS TO DO ALONE

Visit an antiques fair taking something small and not too valuable to sell. Wander round to get an idea of a reasonable price you would accept for it, bearing in mind the dealer has to double it to cover his expenses and make a profit. Ask one of the dealers if he buys things and show him your item. When he asks how much you want for it this is what to say. 'I don't want to haggle, I was told you would offer me a fair price.' This usually works and you get a fair offer.

Merriment

Merriment is not the same as being funny, or just good-natured, and it's not simply the opposite of morose. It's a bubbling sense of fun, of enjoyment, having a mind that works like a radar scanner, constantly finding what in life is pleasing, attractive, and affectionate. Merry people are like hot springs – they constantly bubble up with laughter and delight.

The merriment can be triggered by a remark, a shared memory, a line in a book, almost anything. It has to be shared; like champagne, merriment can't be enjoyed alone. They are not merry the whole time; face set in a rictus grin like a Toby jug, because they too know about reality. But they constantly find new things to bring merriment, to console us for what ails the world.

Most of us are too worried about too many things these days; our jobs, our families, our mortgages, and wider concerns such as terrorism and climate change. Perhaps that's why there is plenty of comedy, but less merriment.

Simon Hoggart, the journalist.

6.
KEEPING WELL, KEEPING HAPPY

Her hair has gone quite gold with grief.

Oscar Wilde

Being a widow is an adventure and to enjoy it you need to be fit and well. To keep well you must keep happy. Research at University College London shows happiness has powerful healing effects on blood pressure, heart disease and inflammation. The writer Fay Weldon claimed that women can never be happy for more than half an hour without worrying about something. Mothers are programmed to worry – it's Darwinian, she says. Have we put the fish away in the fridge, shoud we return the skirt that doesn't fit, have we posted the card to auntie?

To keep well, eat well. You have to eat so make mealtimes a pleasure with good fresh food. Eat food that will rot but not until it's inside you. Take food supplements, extra calcium for bones, garlic tablets and Omega 3 for something or other. Grasp every opportunity to soak up some sun (amply slathered with sun cream of course) and its vitamin D. Many people swear by Echinacea to ward off colds, but it's best to check with your pharmacist to see how any supplements might impact on other medication you're taking. Take a short winter holiday!

Older people need to be warm. Keep the heating on but not too high, it's healthier and cheaper to put on extra clothes. In cold weather dress warmly for outside and in particular keep your neck warm. I am writing this in the middle of winter and the streets are full of people looking miserable in the biting wind because they're wearing Russian boots, ten scarves and no hats. Merry widows need a hat because so much heat is lost through the top of the head. Choose a smart hat such as a fedora or a beret placing them on the front of your head first, not the back. Wear a hat that says, 'Look at me,' not one that says, 'I'm a pathetic old lady trying to be invisible.' You can't be a merry widow shuffling down the street in a woolly pull-on.

On bitter days wear tights under trousers as an extra layer. Cut off the parts of the tights that are supposed to cover the toes and the tights will reach down just above the ankle and out of sight. I belong to a rambling club, we know about these things. Avoid knee-high stockings, they never reach the knees and look ridiculous when you cross your legs, and don't cross your legs, it's bad for circulation. Travel upstairs on buses leaving the coughers and sneezers on the lower deck and wash your hands often.

Cold is inimical to the elderly.

Cicero 65 BC

(I had to look that up: 'inimical' means 'like an enemy').

Lifting heavy weights can damage the muscles in your back. Do not risk it. Stand the legs of tables and chairs in those special plastic cups or fix gliders so they can be pushed instead of lifted; fix casters to small furniture. Garden centres sell plant-stands on casters for moving heavy plants around. Divide garden waste and garbage into separate smaller bags, sometimes the frame of a shopping trolley can be pressed into service for moving heavy loads. What do you do if you buy something and after walking a few yards realise it's too heavy to carry? This calls for ingenuity and struggling home with it is not an option. Go back to the shop and ask them to deliver it for you or call a taxi. You could ask a passing youth to carry it to the bus stop and when you get off the bus leave it somewhere to collect later or ask another youth to carry it home for you. (Be generous with tips; don't save money, save your back). I was in this position having bought a box of one thousand sheets of paper. I called in a hotel and the young man on the desk divided it into two packs for me; there are many kindly people around.

Look after your mental health by keeping cheerful. Do not allow yourself to sit weeping for too long. It is bad for you. Once, after spending ages getting ready for an annual dinner I suddenly realised there was no one downstairs to tell me I looked beautiful. I dried my tears, looked in the hall mirror and said, 'You look utterly fantastic.'

Even if you don't feel like smiling, force your face into the shape of a smile and you will immediately feel better. It really works.

Tiredness can bring on depression so you may have to find time for an afternoon nap in your busy social life. A hot bath in the evening followed by an early night is wonderful for making you feel good.

Some bungalows and apartments are now fitted only with a shower instead of a bath which is a pity because a bath has healing powers.

Everybody gets low sometimes, even happily married people, yes they do. Here are some ways to deal with low spirits.

Your blessings, count them. Think of a few more and count those as well. If people ask how you're feeling say, 'I feel fine,' say it often enough and you'll believe it yourself.

For an interesting exercise look around for a role model. Think of someone who is strong, capable and cheerful and see what you can learn from her but above all learn to be yourself and to like the person you are. Eat chocolate, dark plain chocolate with its high levels of cocoa beans full of antioxidants is now considered to be good for us, not only that, it tastes nice and cheers us up. Listen to Classic FM3, it's lovely music and will alter your mood. Movement also raises the spirit; try dancing to Abba as I suggested and include line dancing or aerobics in your groups. Go for a walk, the longer the better; two hours is better than one hour if you can manage it. Find a route away from traffic noise, a quiet estate will do. To look ten years younger walk tall with a straight back. Walk quickly but not too quickly in case you fall down in the gutter because if they find you there they'll chuck earth over you.

We must look after our health, use moderate exercise,
take just enough food and drink to recover, but not to
overload, our strength. Nor is it the body alone that must
be supported, but the intellect and soul much more. For
they are like lamps, unless you feed them with oil they too
go out.

Cicero (c.65 BC)

No matter how well we look after ourselves, everybody gets
a bit poorly sometimes. If you are worried go to the doctor
or ring NHS Direct, otherwise hide away till you're well
again and tell yourself it will be gone tomorrow. Curries
are good for a cold; they contain so many ingredients one
of them is bound to cure you. Keep a good back-up store
of medicines and check the sell-by date from time to time.
As soon as you feel a little better go for a walk in the fresh
air, it really does help a cold. No matter how much you are
tempted to do so don't talk about illnesses. Nobody wants
to know!

Phoning the stone mason

Me	*'Do you make tombstones?'*
Mason	*'We make memorial headstones, Madam.'*
Me	*'I'd like a grey memorial headstone like the ones in old churchyards.'*
Mason	*'Do you mean Welsh slate?'*
Me	*'Yes, Welsh slate.'*
Mason	*'Set under the ground or on a foundation?'*

Me	'How are the old ones done?'
Mason	'Underground.'
Me	'OK. Underground.'
Mason	'I have to ask if the grave is full.'
Me	'What do you mean?'
Mason	'How many are in it?'
Me	'Only my husband.'
Mason	'Do you mind if I ask whether you are a very tall person?'
Me	'Average height but I'd be lying down. Why does it matter?'
Mason	'A tall person might interfere with the underground foundation'
Me	'You could shunt me along a bit. Will slate look nice?'
Mason	'Very nice indeed. Slate is expensive, it's from Wales like I said and they charge a lot.'
Me	'Could it come from anywhere else?'
Mason	'You can get it from the Continent but it's full of cracks.'
Me	'What did you say?'
Mason	'It's full of cracks.'
Me	'Oh, dear, I thought you said something else.'

7.
FEELING SAFE

Some of your hurts you have cured
And the sharpest you still have survived

But what torments of grief you endured
From evils which never arrived.

Ralph Waldo Emerson, *from Quatrains, borrowed from*
the French

Mobile phones were invented for a merry widow to feel independent and secure in her car as she whizzes round from one social event to another. At the top of your list of names stored in the mobile should be the contact number of your breakdown service or the garage you deal with. Your list is probably in alphabetical order so to make sure this number comes first put A, AA, or AAA in front of it. You may have heard of ICE, short for IN CASE OF EMERGENCY, add this to one of your stored names. In the boot keep a shopping bag, a roll of paper kitchen towels, a blanket and spade for sudden snow and a scraper for icy windows. In summer carry a fold-up cardboard sunscreen for the window.

Now there's no longer somebody around to catch you when you fall take extra care to avoid accidents in the home. People usually fit grip handles and non-slip mats in the bathroom after they have had a fall. Singles must look out for themselves; those fancy bath oils are slippery and if you knock your head and die nobody will find you for a week. And when they do, you'll be naked and frighten the ambulance men.

For reaching up to high places use a lightweight stepladder and keep it handy, not in the garage. Buy a couple of those plastic step stools - the ones with spherical wheels that retract when you stand on the stool - for reaching shelves, one for upstairs and one for down. Take no risks at all with these matters; even a minor accident can spoil your life for a while. If you need to do something difficult, like changing a light bulb at the top of the stairs, wait till someone is with you to hold the ladder.

Watch out for fire; if the phone rings while you're stirring the white sauce, switch everything off or ignore it. There are no phone calls short enough to leave the gas turned on. If it's important they'll ring again and if it's not important they'll ring again.

Concentrate and check the house before you go out. Some keep a list near the front door. 'Oven off, back door locked, heaters off, taps off.' And it is not enough to turn them off; you have to REMEMBER you've turned them off. Imagine sitting in the theatre wondering whether you closed the freezer lid. A good way to remember is to say it aloud as you do it, 'I have switched off my curling tongues.' Buy some timers, keep one next to each electrical appliance and every time you switch on set the timer to ring ten minutes later. If you rely on your memory it will let you down.

If someone is with you when you leave the house it's easy to become harassed and forget things; ask your visitor to wait outside while you check everything.

Think twice before leaving your answerphone switched on. Do you really want to come home with messages to listen to and phone calls to make and pay for? Do you really want to know that nobody called you?

How would you get in if you locked yourself out? Invest in extra keys, hide one somewhere and if you have a friendly neighbour ask if you can leave a key there permanently. Then you could use your mobile to ring from the theatre and ask them to check that freezer lid.

Now here's a funny thing. We all know to watch out for strangers at the door and how to get rid of unwanted callers by keeping a man's cap on show in the hall and by saying, 'I'll have to ask my husband.'

A polite young man came to my door about something or other and as he was leaving he said, 'Could I use your toilet please?' 'Of course,' I answered, letting him in without thinking. It was just the normal reaction and he thanked me politely as he left. We are so friendly and at times so stupid.

Sleep that knits up the ravelled sleeve of care,
Chief nourisher in life's feast...

Shakespeare

Sleeping alone in the house for the first time you may find yourself lying awake nervously listening for noises: pipes cooling down - axe murderers etc. Pitter-pat of rain on the window - four burglars creeping upstairs. Be rational about this, every house has its noises. If you were having a rest on the bed in the afternoon you wouldn't be afraid, so what is the difference? Darkness is the difference, get rid of it. Keep lights on everywhere; buy low-wattage bulbs for upstairs rooms. This anxious feeling will soon wear off and in the meantime what's more important, peace of mind or your electricity bill? Incidentally low-wattage bulbs can be left on all day if you're coming home late; they're too weak to show up in daylight but look bright and welcoming after dark.

Oprah Winfrey, of the American chat show, says we should all have a plan in case we think there is an intruder. She suggested having something at hand to make a great noise, perhaps a couple of saucepan lids. What about a loud whistle or a recording of a dog barking loudly? Or a real dog?

You may have trouble getting to sleep. We are used to a warm, breathing, familiar body next to ours. The widow's bed is an unwelcoming place and going to bed at all in the early weeks is something to dread as we slide under the sheets, snap the light off and hope morning comes pretty damn quick.

Your first priority is to make the bedroom into a cosy haven that's all your own. Create a place to look forward to at bedtime. Begin by clearing away all the man things from the room. On the dressing-table arrange a pretty display of perfume bottles under soft lighting together with a tea tray.

At the bedside keep magazines, a radio and a notebook for those jobs you remember just as you doze off.

To help you sleep better have the window open a little even on cold nights and avoid anything worrying late in the evening. We're not obliged to watch the ten o'clock news every night, our grandmothers didn't have the world's misery at their firesides: crime, wars, earthquakes. Switch it all off and listen to classical music or something funny.

A widow speaks - *I used to wake in the night and wonder where he was.*

It's best not to eat a lot before bedtime but a hot milky drink will help you sleep and so will a thimble full of whisky. Winston Churchill said whisky was man's greatest consolation. A merry widow friend tells me that brandy is even better, taken last thing at night in hot milk. I asked how much hot milk, 'You put the hot milk in the brandy and not the other way round,' she joked. This is the same friend who warned me off sherry saying it was easy to become addicted. Sherry tastes good she said and, because it can be enjoyed at lunchtimes, we don't notice how strong it is. This lady is an expert on matters alcoholic because she was an army wife and much travelled. She says champagne is the perfect drink, because although the nice feeling soon wears off, it is the only drink that does not cause a hangover; she knows about hangovers as well.

In summer you may need to block out the light to prevent waking too early. In winter a pillow down the bed lengthways will keep the draught out and bring comfort through the night. With one of his jumpers to cuddle up to, you will soon be off. By the way, don't wash the jumper. Widows often dream of their husbands and occasionally experience something called a presence when he seems to visit them.

I have never believed in ghosts and once, on a graveyard project with some students, one of them asked the gravedigger if he had ever seen a ghost. This was his reply:

'In forty years of working in this cemetery I've never seen a ghost. It's the living you have to be afraid of my dear, not the dead.'

One night, about two weeks after my husband's funeral, I dreamed he was standing in the lounge on the spot where he had the fall that led to his last illness. He put his arms round me. I felt the rough tweed of his jacket, the softness of his face, the warmth of his breath and an overwhelming sense of everything being right again. I said, 'You can't do this, you're dead,' and he was gone. It was much more vivid than a dream because there was dimension and solidity. I felt it was his way of letting me know he was still looking after me.

So although I don't believe in ghosts there may be harmless little spirits around that our conscious brain is not equipped to recognise. Who is to say? Literature and religion are full of references to spirits.

We really know nothing about the true persistence of the soul and the continuation of life and the rhythms between death and life.

A widow speaks - *I felt that he was still in the house for about five weeks after he died. One night the portable radio in the kitchen came on and although I was really frightened I went downstairs. It was on very loud. I switched it off, went back to bed and it came on again. I thought it was something to do with the battery. I don't know why it came on. Perhaps it was his way of telling me he was all right.*

8.
GO FOR COMEDY
GO FOR CULTURE

To keep happy go for comedy. Merry widows love to laugh. Ronnie Barker, Tommy Cooper, we watch them over and over. Why? Because they make us laugh and laughter is essential for good health. Laughter boosts our immune system helping us to stay well. Comedy is not trivial, comedy is medicine.

Glance through any TV listings and the word 'comedy' will immediately attract the viewer and there are never enough of these programs to meet demand. Every night at 6.30pm there is something light on Radio 4; people have come home from work, listened to the six o'clock news and are ready for their spirits to be lifted by something funny. Comedy gives another perspective on the world, a different way of looking at things. If you can make a joke about a serious matter it takes away the sting and empowers us.

People stop me in the street and solemnly ask, 'How are you getting on?'

'Fine,' is my usual reply, 'no shirts to iron.' They look taken aback and sometimes rather disappointed but it makes me feel better. Comedy is a serious business and born of adversity. Jewish humour is famous. It comes from two thousand years of oppression.

> *'Knock knock'.*
> *'Who's there?'*
> *'Are you the widow Cohen?'*
> *'Of course not.'*
> *'Have I got news for you!'*

Things can be said in jokes that cannot otherwise easily be said. Schoolboys give funny nicknames to teachers they fear because it gives the child the upper hand. Comedy has power.

At the time of the war in Vietnam when US soldiers were being killed and people demanded an end to the fighting, a satirical song became extremely popular in America.

> *… 'Be the first on the block*
> *To have your boy come home in a box.'*

The US government tried to ban it but the song helped to end the war. Comedy confronts tragedy head on.

A dirty, foulmouthed old man lives in squalor with his forty-year-old bachelor son. The son, with neither talent nor great intelligence, aspires to an intellectual life of elegant living. He blames his father for standing in the way of achieving this better life but in reality the son does not have the courage or imagination to change anything. The stuff of tragedy you may think, but this is the scenario for *Steptoe and Son*, the enormously popular sitcom of the 1960s and 1970s.

Comedy is the bedfellow of tragedy. Seek out laughter and look for the funny side of things.

> *Do like other widows, buy yourself weeds and be*
> *cheerful.*

John Gay The Beggar's Opera

Whenever I heard the phrase 'Culture and the Arts' I used to feel like running to hide in a cupboard in case somebody was forcing me to enjoy myself. This was a foolish reaction because millions of pounds of tax-payers' money goes into subsidising cultural activities such as art, music and theatre. We need beauty as much as we need bread and all that is fine and beautiful finds its expression in the arts. A cultural interest is life enhancing and being widowed is a wonderful opportunity to develop and explore these interests.

Listening to music and going to concerts puts us in touch with emotions we share with the rest of humanity and is vital for mental health. Opera evokes these emotions most deeply and can also evoke emotions we were unaware of. 'Nessun Dorma' sung by Pavarotti did not come top of the charts that year merely because of the football. Music expands our horizons beyond the workaday world. It doesn't matter if we don't know the composer or the title; it's the listening that matters. At a classical concert when everything is in harmony, the grandeur of the hall and the stilled concentration of rows of people, music can carry us to another place, a place beyond, a place sublime. All art has the potential to change mood and lift the human spirit in this way.

Serious concertgoers concentrate on the music all the time but a merry widow may find her mind wandering. She may wonder why the men in the orchestra look so smart in their dinner jackets while the women look funereal, dressed in unrelieved black. Why can't they wear pretty clothes? And why does the conductor keep going off and coming on again at the end and how does he know when to stop coming back?

A friend sings in a choir and she speaks of other members as if they were her family. If she has to miss a weekly rehearsal she's devastated. When I asked how it felt to be in a choir she said it was exhilarating, 'I sing alto and can hear the tenors nearby, the music and the voices are thrilling.' I must say I am rather envious of this part of her life.

A widow speaks - *I used to sing all the time, in the kitchen or standing on the stairs. After a year of being bereaved I realised I hadn't sung a note. Now my voice is not so strong but I sometimes find myself singing. People don't decide to sing, it just comes upon them when they are happy.*

Certain activities can be enjoyed much more without the distraction of a companion and a visit to an art exhibition is one of them. In a strange town head for the art gallery; it's usually free, there'll be interesting people in the gift shop and probably a good restaurant. Just wandering round and lingering over the pictures you like will furnish your mind with great images. Spend time actually looking; months and months of work by an artist cannot be appreciated in a few seconds. If there's a guided tour, tag on to it, nobody has the nerve to challenge an older lady; we can do what we like, and save the catalogue till you get home, you've come to look, not to read.

Some rooms in art galleries have long upholstered seats. These have been placed there for merry widows to put their shopping down and have a short rest while contemplating the inauguration of a pope in medieval Venice covering the wall opposite. The pope in his golden chair and rows of cardinals in scarlet are spread before you exactly as the artist saw them five hundred years ago. Every detail. And now you are seeing what he saw. That is amazing. And when you leave the gallery you carry the picture with you and that is even more amazing; fine art stays in the mind.

Be open to modern art. Although much of it is pretentious and a splodge is still a splodge and a six-metre square of blue paint is just so much Dulux, modern art exhibitions can deliver works that are exciting and surprising. Unusual forms of art have something to offer the merry widow with time on her hands. I recently followed a sign pointing to something called a video installation and found myself sitting in a dark room in front of a ten-metre screen divided into three sections. The theme was cameras and tourism. The first section showed a famous European city, the second a close up of the architecture and the third showed tourists taking photos of each other. Every two minutes the scene changed to a different city, different close up and different tourists; altogether it lasted about half an hour.

A memorable experience. Before leaving an art gallery ask the staff where they go for lunch.

Going out to professional theatre is usually worth all the trouble and expense of booking seats and getting there. Dressing up at leisure is part of the pleasure and so is the delight of mingling with people in the foyer and saying hello to someone you know. It is not only what is on the stage that makes it such a splendid way for a merry widow to spend an evening. We've all seen mouldy plays in our time but when it's a good one and the actors carry us away, theatre can be tremendous.

Warm day? Be prepared for the arctic blast called air-conditioning by carrying a cardigan and take a small bottle of water to save queuing at the interval.

In a bad seat? Look round for a better one and sit in it. If the first act is tedious be assured the second half will be no better; leave at the interval and go shopping.

If you're with a group of people and don't want to offend the organiser, find out what time the play finishes then creep back in near the end. A good clue to a disappointing play is a tray of drinks on the stage; it's there to give actors something diverting to do while they talk and talk and talk. Other plays to beware of are those written solely for a famous TV star where the attraction is not the play but the star. The U3A groups, mentioned in the section on friends, often organise trips to cultural events but keep an eye open as well for details of concerts and exhibitions in your own area. Pick up leaflets in libraries and read notices in shop windows; some of these local events are of an excellent standard.

My particular interest is poetry and I have reason to be grateful for this interest. When the message came that my dear one had died I sat in the taxi determined to be brave and dreading what I was about to see. What a shock to find him lying there, behind the curtained cubicle, looking angry. His lips were pressed into a thin line, his jaw was set in an expression of fury and the cold waxen hand I stroked as it lay on top of the sheet was fiercely clenched into a fist. His whole attitude was one of reproach.

Something was not right. I had thought people passed away peacefully and expected him to be lying there as if he was asleep. Beyond distress I wandered bewildered into the hospital grounds. The poor man. How could a person be dead and look so angry? Into my mind came the lines of a poem by Dylan Thomas:

'Do not go gentle into that good night
Old age should burn and rave at close of day;
Rage, rage against the dying of the light.'

Nothing else in the world could have helped me at that moment, no arm round the shoulder and no words of comfort could have given the enormous consolation of those lines. Such is the purpose of poetry. Everything fell into place and I felt a strange sense of pride at the strength of his protest. Fine words and the arts have practical value. Go for culture.

Could we even know each other in the slightest without the arts?

Gabriel Roy (writer), quoted on the Canadian $20 bill.

FUN THINGS TO DO
WHEN NOBODY IS LOOKING

- Walk barefoot on wet grass

- Pick a violet

- Blow a kiss to a lorry driver on the crossing.

GRAVESIDE

Cremation was never an option for my dear one; he said enough people in his family had been burnt by the Nazis. With no intention of making a career out of it I sometimes visit the grave, perhaps taking a few flowers from his garden or even an apple from his tree. He lies in an ancient graveyard not far from a buddleia bush where Red Admirals gather near a Bronze Age burial site.

On my first visit after the funeral the only other people there were a man and woman talking loudly to each other a few feet away from the grave. I waited, hoping they would go away but they went on and on, discussing all the people they had once worked with. I had gone there to spend a quiet time but it was just not possible. There they stood, ignoring me in spite of my increasingly glaring glances. Thinking an interruption might bring their chat to a close, I asked if they could tell me where I could collect some water.

'Over there,' the man said, 'and you'll find a plastic bottle to carry it in.'

I fetched some water, which I didn't need, and they were still there. Then I had a bright idea. If I knelt by the grave pretending to pray they would be bound to go away; no normal person would carry on talking while someone nearby was at prayer. Finding a space on the rubble between the floral wreathes, I knelt for a few minutes. Even that did not work and I was getting more and more angry and frustrated.

I thought of my dear one lying below like a medieval prince in his wicker coffin and burgundy gown and wondered what he would have done. He would have told them to bugger off. So I did. 'Excuse me, I wonder if you would be kind enough to move away and talk somewhere else. I would like a quiet time with my husband.'

'Oh, all right,' they said gormlessly and wandered off.

The Walk

You did not walk with me
Of late to the hill-top tree
By the gated ways,
As in earlier days;
You were weak and lame,
So you never came,
And I went alone, and I did not mind,
Not thinking of you as left behind.

I walked up there today
Just in the former way:
Surveyed around
The familiar ground
By myself again:
What difference then?
Only that underlying sense
Of the look of a room on returning thence.

Thomas Hardy

9.

SOLO HOUSEKEEPING

You'd think a house with only one person in it would be easy to run. However, Merry widows soon discover housekeeping for singles is no pushover. Everything he did is now up to you; washing up, putting out milk bottles, cooking, defrosting the freezer, altering clocks, dealing with bills, and on and on goes the list. All these jobs are now yours alone.

But how can you be merry if you wear yourself out with housework? Go easy, perfection is not your aim. Practise being a slut. Dust once a month whether it needs it or not. The inimitable Quentin Crisp said that after five years dust doesn't get any thicker. Wash up once a day, stack them on the drainer, rinse them in cold water, not hot, cover them with a tea towel and in the morning everything will be sparkling like new. Store cling film and baking foil in a shallow top drawer, pulling out a few inches ready for use before closing it. For freshness keep floor cloths outside the back door instead of in the kitchen. To save a lot of dashing up and down keep an extra vacuum cleaner in a spare bedroom and, if you regularly answer the phone up there, keep your diary half way up the stairs.

It's difficult to do when you're busy but to be tidy put things away straight away. By keeping shelves, tables and work surfaces clear of all clutter the whole room will have that just-cleaned look. Consider employing somebody to help with the cleaning even if it's only once a fortnight. A cleaner is company and somebody to call on if you are ill or need the house looking after while you're away enjoying yourself. Ask friends for a recommendation; and try not to clean up before she comes. If it's a choice between gardener and cleaner, a gardener is better because he'll do heavy jobs like lifting and it's good to have a man around. While he does all the spadework you can grow sweet peas and carry them in a trug basket like a lady. Fresh flowers bring joy to the spirit; display some in the kitchen where you can see them. Do nice things like this for yourself, you're worth it.

Every time you pass a mirror give your muscles a face-lifting workout. Twist your face into weird, weird shapes till it hurts, finishing with your hardest smile, first one side then the other. For a smoother neck, chin down, open your mouth wide, head back, close the mouth. Does all this work? You'll soon see.

Merry widows don't hoard jewellery.

If you never wear it give it away; a piece of jewellery will mean much more to somebody if it's given before you die. Dip it in methylated spirits for sparkle before presenting it in a smart box with a birthday card, 'My intention was to will this to you but I'd like you to have it now.' They'll love you forever and weep at your funeral. Do be sure you've finished with it, you can't ask for it back and it does not matter if you never see them wearing it.

Clear out your wardrobe to make space for lovely new clothes. Merry widows love fashion and few things make you look older than wearing out-of-date clothes but without granddaughters it's difficult to know what's in. Fashion matters, it's the pulse of the universe. Study window displays or watch young people as they walk by, particularly fourteen year olds, they're the experts. Fashions do sometimes come back in but they are never exactly the same so it's no good hanging on to things from the last decade. Study the details of TV shows with characters dressed as fussy old ladies. (Yes, there are rather a lot of them). Look at her outfit, look at hair, look at earrings, look at make-up; that's what not to wear.

Think carefully before spending a lot of money on clothes. The most elegant woman I know tells me she has very few outfits. She wears dresses instead of separates and never minds being seen in the same ones more than once. As long as you look nice she says it doesn't matter and nobody notices anyway.

Certain garments give a merry widow instant style. One is a tailored jacket in a plain dark colour, usually black, teamed with that other staple – a crisp white shirt. Because it gives shape and definition to the body a jacket always looks smart. In summer a short-sleeved unlined jacket with slim shoulder pads has the same effect. In winter a plain black woollen top worn with pearls, or a bright silk scarf, also looks terrific.

Another essential for the merry widow is a pair of fine leather gloves to flutter as she waves across the street to friends.

Keep a list behind the wardrobe door of when clothes were last cleaned, we become a bit forgetful and merry widows must be fragrant on all occasions. Use steam from a kettle to freshen up a hat or jacket. Clothes that don't need washing till you've worn them a few more times can be aired overnight before hanging them inside out in the wardrobe as a reminder. Keep skirts, tops, dresses and trousers in their own separate section on the rail. Stitch hanging loops to trousers. Transform a long-sleeved blouse that you never wear by cutting off the sleeves to make them short. I know these things; I once worked in a dress factory. Garments from man-made fibres need washing more often than wool and cotton. That's another thing, your laundry basket will be nowhere near as full without his towels and shirts and if you place a sheet between you and the duvet you will save even more wash loads.

Wash some clothes by hand; they look better for it, especially woollens, and last much longer. Remember not to use biological detergents on silk and wool. What I'd like to know is how long to keep an odd sock in case the other one turns up.

Charity shops were invented to stop merry widows feeling guilty about throwing clothes away, so if you haven't worn something for a year take it to a charity shop. While you're in there have a look round; there's always potential for an exciting surprise such as a quality blouse with a back yoke and collar set on a band.

Be ruthless with shoes, if they hurt a bit, or are out of fashion, charity shop. Blu-tack will remove marks from pale suede and some sandals can actually be washed.

At the end of each season put a few clothes away and you'll have a surprise when the year comes round again.

Use lavender sprigs instead of moth balls, they do the same job.

When you feel ready, which may be many months after his death, gradually make decisions about his belongings. There will be certain items that mean a lot to you, perhaps some clothing or things he treasured. I will never dispose of his best jacket, for instance, nor the small items that came back from the hospital including keys, a magnifying glass, and for some reason, a Royal Army Ordnance Corps cap badge. I keep them in a special drawer and one day I may bring myself to spend the three pounds twenty pence in his purse.

A lovely idea is to wear some of his clothes yourself; I wear his warm pyjama top as a bed-jacket. In a small box I have a lock of his black hair which I saved when he began to go grey. Victorians ladies saved locks of hair in gold lockets on necklaces. It certainly feels pleasant to touch the hair of a dear departed one.

Keeping on one side those things you cannot bear to part with, lay the rest out on a spare bed, and say to people who visit, 'Please take anything you like from here.' I thought relatives and friends might like some of his clothing. I was wrong. In the end it all went to charity shops except for a pair of new sandals, which a friend asked for, and I'm delighted to see him wearing them.

You may need to be selective in your memories. People are not themselves when they are ill and if he needed your care for a long time making life difficult and distressing for you, distance yourself from it. Cut it all off. Push it away.

Get rid of anything in the home that reminds you of these times. Take pride in whatever care you gave and fill your heart with memories of the good years.

Do your bit for the planet and for your health. Walk to the shops instead of driving, but not with a four-wheeled shopping trolley because you'll look a hundred years old. There's nothing wrong with being old but nobody wants to look a hundred, unless of course you happen to be a hundred and two. Buy a baby's pushchair from Argos, plonk a smart bag on it and go shopping, it will carry a week's groceries whizzing up pavements and round corners making you feel young and jaunty. Nobody notices there's not a baby in it, except other babies and the look of puzzlement on their little faces is a delight. There's a fortune waiting for a company that brings out a smart shopping trolley perhaps with some power built in, especially if it's advertised with a celebrity pushing it down the street. You read it here first.

Still on shopping, instead of carrying a shopping bag use a smart plastic one from a top department store; you'll look as if you've just bought something new on an impulse. If you must shop with a car display a panama hat in the back window, it looks so elegant.

On a wet day clear out some of your lifetime collection of photographs. You will of course live forever, but if by chance you don't, your relatives will take the whole lot to the council tip.

Sepia photos of the 1920s and 1930s embossed with the name of the studio are small works of art, save them. At one time only the wealthy had cameras and people made appointments with a photographer's studio for pictures of new babies lying naked on their tummies, (you'd be in trouble for that nowadays) or family groups with mother seated, father behind and children standing at the side, all looking composed and serene. Save all these but on the back write the names of the people with dates. These go in a strong brown envelope labelled, 'Family pictures to keep'. If there's a relative interested in family history now would a good time to pass them on. Be ruthless with all the coloured snaps of people grinning on beaches, throw them away but rip them up first otherwise they may be published in the local paper under the heading

'Has any reader lost this photograph?'

A word of caution. This type of activity where you look back over the years can be depressing so do it with a glass of wine and for no longer than half an hour at a time.

A widow speaks - *My husband died fifteen years ago and we had a lovely marriage but I've never been as happy as I am now.*

Reorganize the toolbox, you're the handyman now; perhaps you always were. Merry widows enjoy fixing things. A favourite tool is a T-shaped awl, which looks like a very thin corkscrew. This is for making holes in wood prior to fixing a screw. Other essentials are a metal pull out tape measure and a long straight edge (either a metal ruler or a strip of carpet edging.)

There's a splendid product called No More Nails that comes in a big tube and really works; you can fix a shelf to a wall without using a drill or screws. Also in the toolbox keep a roll of waterproof duct tape. This wide silver tape will repair many things including a plastic roof. Duct tape will also remove warts, a doctor told me this so it must be true.

Be ready to deal with a spider. If it's in the bath open the window wide, grab a towel, gently fold your visitor into it and shake him through the window. If he's running along the carpet, cover him with a glass mug, slide a piece of card underneath and carry it outside. Be brave. You can do it if you don't look it in the eye.

THE WATER METER MAN AND I

Scene	*My kitchen*
WMM	*'All finished. I've fixed your water meter and if you're careful you'll save a lot of money now you're alone.'*
ME	*'Thank you, I've wanted that doing for ages.'*
WMM`	*'Just sign here and I'll be on my way.'*
ME	*'When will it start metering?'*
WMM	*'It's started already.'*
ME	*'But I've just given you a cup of coffee!'*

10.

FOOD GLORIOUS FOOD

Fate cannot harm me, I have dined well today.

Sydney Smith

Two is the ideal number for dinner,
me and a good head waiter.

Author unknown

First you lose your husband then you lose your appetite. Huddled in the kitchen over something on toast is no way for a widow to become merry. Good food is essential for a sense of well-being, to combat depression and to keep you healthy and happy. If you have no energy for anything else cook a dainty meal, pour a glass of wine and sit at a properly laid table in your best clothes and full make-up.

Preparing a meal for yourself is something to look forward to and, although there are some wonderful ready-made meals on supermarket shelves, home-cooked food is better. Buy top quality ingredients; cheap food is cheap food. Cooking is a creative activity, cook for six, not six people but six servings and store them in the freezer ready for when you come get home after a fun evening. You will need to label your freezer packs of cooked food clearly because a pack of frozen raspberries looks similar to tomato soup.

Here's a quick soup. Stir half a pint of chicken cube stock into a tin of chopped tomatoes. That's it. Another idea for a quick meal is to buy a box of eight cooked chicken legs from M&S and freeze them separately ready to eat cold or steamed over a pan of boiling potatoes.

Organise yourself. In your kitchen keep a bay leaf plant; one leaf will flavour a stew and one in the cabbage water will prevent unpleasant smells. You'll have to replace the plant from time to time because once it's down to five leaves it gives up. Buy a good quality sliced loaf, store it in separate slices in the freezer and you will always have fresh bread. Buy a wine box for drawing off a glassful at a time and for adding to stews or use a simple vacuum stopper to make a bottle of wine last ages.

You will soon discover two things about catering for one. The grocery bill goes down because men eat more and you will sometimes have to throw food away. This is painful for those brought up to economise but there's no alternative if you bought too much. And you will buy too much. Eggs and hot cross buns come in packs of six; you hardly eat any bread at all and you have no appetite for the left-over pie that looked so delicious on the packet. The boiled potatoes you saved in the fridge for tomorrow and tomorrow and tomorrow will also eventually be thrown away. Get used to it.

At one time there was something puritanical about the English attitude to food. I was raised not to speak about the meal on the table because that was a sign of gluttony. But they were the days of food rationing and food was unspeakable anyway. Until quite recently most people did not go out for meals. On a long car journey in 1976, often, the only place open on a Sunday for food was a hotel where all the tables were reserved for residents. Thankfully all is different now and dining out in good restaurants is a form of entertainment. It is wonderful to see whole families, including babies, enjoying Sunday lunch, a meal that used to take hours for the mother to cook. Cafes and restaurants are a pleasure to all, especially the merry widow who would otherwise be eating alone at home.

Take a book with you.

At least once a week plan a meal out with a friend; many pubs have terrific lunch deals; ask around for the best places. Lunching with friends is a fine thing to look forward to and costs about the same as eating at home without all the palaver. Take your diary and at the end of the meal plan the next one. Before long you will have the great pleasure of a lunching out routine.

If you enjoy entertaining you can occasionally invite two or three people, including a fat bloke (see later) for a meal, don't call it 'dinner' or it might put you off doing it. Suggest a time for their visit, perhaps seven till nine-thirty; people like to know where they stand. If you invite guests it will give you the motivation to make your house look special but have all the cleaning done in advance leaving a whole day with nothing to do except prepare the meal and make yourself look nice.

Doing everything alone takes a lot of confidence but it's easy if you avoid stress by keeping it simple. Your guests won't expect a banquet and this is no time to show off your culinary skills. In any case if you make a meal that's too elaborate it will put them off asking you back.

A well-laid table is a thing of beauty and a great appetiser so set it the day before. Take your best glasses, cutlery and plates out checking each piece as you arrange it because crockery can lose its shine just by sitting in a sideboard for a few months. A lace cloth is attractive for evenings or you can polish the table and have no cloth at all. Red serviettes look festive and so do candles and flowers, but keep the flower arrangement small or it could interfere with conversation. An elegant touch is a small hand-written menu. Dear reader, you know all this, I'm just giving you the confidence to do it without a husband. It's great to realise we can do these things without him.

Plan a meal that keeps you out of the kitchen as much as possible such as a cold starter, one hot main course and a cold dessert. Buy a terrific pudding as well. Cook the main dish a few days in advance ready to heat up; a cottage pie perhaps, with crisp mashed potato on top, or beef in Guinness. Men love this sort of food and it often tastes even better warmed up. Remember to check the flavour just before serving. Sprinkle it generously with chopped parsley or parsley sprigs; place it in the middle of the table with a colourful salad and they'll think you're wonderful. Jeffrey Archer's parties were famous; all he served was champagne and shepherd's pie, which he cooked himself.

Have some music playing in the background when they come, Strauss waltzes are welcoming, and keep a vase handy in case they bring flowers; it's a nuisance having to interrupt everything to deal with fresh flowers. If your guests bring wine you do not have to serve it at the table, save it for next time. When they arrive you could offer sherry or a glass of the wine you're having for dinner. Bucks Fizz is another alternative to drink beforehand. These days many people, especially if they're driving, prefer not to take alcohol at all so prepare a jug of iced water with slices of lemon and leaves of mint. If they offer to help, let them; you could ask a man to serve the wine or light the candles.

Guests may be hungry when they arrive, so once people are seated at the table serve the first course promptly then take your time over the rest of the meal, chatting at leisure between courses. If you feel that moving away for coffee would break up the conversation serve coffee at the dining table instead. Relax and make the most of having company in the house and if anything goes wrong make light of it, 'The same thing happened that time Her Majesty came.'

Sometimes friends offer to wash up, say no at first and if they persist say ten minutes would be helpful. Give them an apron and rubber gloves while you do the clearing up because they'll be happier at the sink. It is amazing how easy it is with two of you. We remember, don't we girls? When it's time to leave wait till they're right out of sight before closing the front door (pop a coat on in winter.)

A word of advice. You need guests with a good appetite. My first lunch party was disappointing because I had invited three women and women don't eat much. Feeding a hungry man is a real pleasure to a merry widow. Invite a fat bloke.

DIARY

In a supermarket queue I asked an Indian lady with six melons in her basket if she was having a party. It was the first anniversary of her husband's death she explained and their custom was to have a memorial party. That sounded an excellent idea and I made small photocopied invitations for 'tea and cake,' to hand round to rambling friends. They were asked to ring if they were coming; I didn't say what the occasion was in case they felt obliged to be sad.

What a delightful sound is the exciting chatter of a crowd in my garden on a Sunday afternoon, and how foolish I'd been that morning to think it was all too much and wishing I hadn't invited them at all.

Twenty-three people came, and, ignoring my newly-polished lounge, they marched straight through carrying dining chairs, stools and anything else they could find to sit on outside.

Cakes that could be eaten with fingers were laid out in the kitchen and they helped themselves as they came in to collect a cup of tea.

A perfect afternoon from which I learnt two valuable lessons; a big group is easier to manage than a small one because they don't need entertaining and widows need to think carefully before disposing of any surplus cups and saucers; they may well be needed.

Bereft

In the black winter morning
No light will be struck near my eyes
While the clock in the stairway is warning
For five, when he used to rise.
Leave the door unbarred
The clock unwound.
Make my lone bed hard -
Would 'twere underground!

When the summer dawns clearly,
And the appletree-tops seem alight
Who will draw the curtain and cheerly
Call out that the morning is bright?

When I tarry at market
No form will cross Durnover Lea
In the gathering darkness, to hark at
Grey's Bridge for the pit-pat o'me.

When the supper crock's steaming
And the time is the time of his tread,
I shall sit by the fire and wait dreaming
In a silence as of the dead.
Leave the door unbarred
The clock unwound.
Make my lone bed hard -
Would 'twere underground!

Thomas Hardy

11.
GOING PLACES

It's all very well reading books like this and being brave and strong and not giving in but merry widows need holidays. Getting away brings a new perspective and what seemed a major worry in your kitchen becomes a mere trifle in a hotel overlooking the sea. Short trips, not too close together, are best.

The right holiday will transform and brighten your life; an experience to look forward to and enjoy talking about afterwards. As well as the opportunity to meet new people and explore new places, holidays have the potential for excitement and adventure.

Widows discover that memories of holidays spent with the dear one are the most precious memories of all. Perhaps it's photographs that make recall so poignant or merely the memory of being happy together in lovely settings. Whatever the reason, it is not a good idea to revisit places you both enjoyed. Thomas Hardy did and wrote a very beautiful poem about it called 'After a Journey'.

After a Journey

Hereto I come to view a voiceless ghost;
  Whither, O whither will its whim now draw me?

Up the cliff, down, till I'm lonely, lost,
  And the unseen waters' ejaculations awe me.
Where you will next be there's no knowing,
  Facing round about me everywhere,
    With your nut-coloured hair,
And gray eyes, and rose-flush coming and going.
Yes: I have re-entered your olden haunts at last;
  Through the years, through the dead scenes I have
tracked you;
What have you now found to say of our past -

Scanned across the dark space wherein I have lacked you?
Summer gave us sweets, but autumn wrought
division?
  Things were not lastly as firstly well
    With us twain, you tell?
But all's closed now, despite Time's derision.
I see what you are doing: you are leading me on
  To the spots we knew when we haunted here
together,
The waterfall, above which the mist-bow shone
  At the then fair hour in the then fair weather,
And the cave just under, with a voice still so hollow
That it seems to call out to me from forty years ago,
    When you were all aglow,
And not the thin ghost that I now fraily follow!
Ignorant of what there is flitting here to see,
  The waked birds preen and the seals flop lazily;
Soon you will have, Dear, to vanish from me,
  For the stars close their shutters and the dawn
whitens hazily.

Trust me, I mind not, though Life lours,
  The bringing me here; nay, bring me here again!
    I am just the same as when
Our days were a joy, and our paths through flowers.
Pentargan Bay

What a lovely poem! But poetry is poetry, and reality is reality, and I'm here to teach you how to be a merry widow.

So don't imagine you can't have a great holiday now that your husband is no longer with you!

After all, don't you think your husband still wants you to have a great holiday even though he can't share it with you anymore?

Because the grass doesn't grow, winter is a good time to go away leaving the warm summer months to enjoy gardens and the English countryside.

For peace of mind secure your house. My plumber tells me to set the heating low and turn the water off because he has seen the damage burst pipes can do. Use your friendly low-wattage bulbs switched on all the time or set time switches. Small things make a house look occupied, something hanging on the line for instance or unwashed pots in the kitchen (if you can bear it). Leave your car on the drive instead of the garage or ask a neighbour to park their car outside your house.

If you feel OK travelling alone, go for an activity holiday, such as bird-watching or photography. These special-interest holidays are ideal for people on their own because you immediately have something in common with everybody you meet there. People tend to leave couples alone but they will soon start talking to single travellers.

In the early months, widows are usually happier going away with a group of people they know. Some of the new organisations you join may arrange holidays. What could be better than boarding a coach full of familiar faces all saying hello? You share the fun of being together as well as the strength of the group if things go wrong, though most likely they won't.

My favourite holidays are with a local walking group that organises two UK weekend coach trips a year. Breakfast, dinner and packed lunch in a good class hotel and dancing or games in the evening are all included if you want them. On Friday and Monday there's a short walk en route and on Saturday and Sunday there is a choice of walks. Non-walkers have the option of visits to nearby towns and places of interest all by coach. It is no surprise that people join this organisation solely for these weekends away.

In the interests of conserving energy, the Bishop of London has declared that flying is a sin. He may be right. Airports are a penance for our wickedness. That's why we must wake in the middle of the night to arrive three hours before take-off, queue for check-in, shuffle through a cattle pen called security where we have to take many of our clothes off and submit to a body scan. What I want to know is, does this also happen to first-class passengers? Just wondered.

For air travel an aisle seat is best as you won't have to disturb anybody when you go sprinting round for exercise.

Take a paperback, anything will do; not for reading but to stop people talking to you, unless he's handsome. Don't rely on a magazine; you'll have read it all by the time you've taxied to the runway.

If your ears become blocked on landing hold your nose, close your mouth and blow gently, or chew a mint or gum.

Set two alarm clocks for an early start. Set your mobile as well, it will terrify you as it rattles on the dressing table but you'll wake up. If you're travelling with a friend, ask her to ring you when she wakes. You probably won't need any of this because you'll be too excited to sleep.

Learn about the place beforehand by contacting the local tourist office or using the internet. You need at least a plan of the town and a list of its attractions. Find out if the hotel supplies hair dryers or tea-making facilities (most continental hotels do not.) A travelling kettle or a cup boiler is a great comfort especially if you were sensible enough to pay extra for a single room. Merry widows need to be alone if they've been with a group all day and even with a group keep your independence by going off on your own sometimes. Don't be a clinger. If you are going out alone at night ask at reception if it's safe and carry something with the name of your hotel on in case you forget; it happens; it happens to young people too. Cross the road ONLY AT PROPER CROSSING PLACES because they all drive on the wrong side and if a truck knocks you down you won't be missed for a week. By the way, bear in mind that in some countries eg. the Czech Republic trams have the right of way even at pedestrian crossings. By remembering this you can avoid joining your husband prematurely.

'Travel light,' we are advised but it doesn't work. Having cleverly crammed a week's luggage into a small case the taxi driver expected me to hoist it up into the boot without help. In the hotel my case was left in the lobby after everyone else's had gone. It was so small they assumed I'd be taking it up myself. Travel light but not too light.

Consider doing your packing downstairs because when the case is full it may be too heavy to carry down.

The worst thing about packing is thinking about it so make decisions a few days before. Put on one side your complete travelling outfit including the comfortable shoes you will be wearing, remembering that holidays involve lots of walking about.

Dear reader, if you are wondering whether going away without him is worth all this trouble – it is.

Starting from the feet up lay out the rest of your clothes on a spare bed and start eliminating. If in doubt leave it out. Take only your favourite things and it helps to stick to one or two basic colours. I once went to America with clothes that were all either royal blue or white. It worked, even if the photographs were a touch monotonous. Pack underwear that you've had in your drawer for too long, wear it on holiday, then throw it away and buy new things when you come home. Make use of the hotel laundry for blouses. You won't need half the makeup you normally use, and sugar from a hotel dining room makes a great facial scrub. In your hand-luggage pack spare underwear and a tooth brush just in case your luggage lands up somewhere with a name like Elan Baffleur.

Handbags are a nuisance for air travel, men don't carry them; they use pockets instead. Pack your handbag and for the journey wear a man's sleeveless cotton jacket. These beige garments have lots of zipped pockets for your passport, tickets and other documents and make life more secure for the lone traveller. A handbag is a worry, you are forever rummaging in it and if you leave it anywhere it's a disaster.

Tie a brightly coloured scarf or cloth round your case, not a pretty bit of ribbon but something big and gaudy. You need to be able to spot your luggage easily among the hundred similar cases gliding past on the carousel. Never mind if it doesn't look elegant; your bag will not be picked up by mistake and nobody will nick it. Stand next to a strong man as the case passes by and ask him nicely if he'll lift it off for you. No need to be shy, most men like to be asked for help.

Take a photocopy of your passport and carry a spiral notebook. In the front section make a note of the phone number and details (not pin number) in case you lose your credit card. Also in the book go names, addresses and phone numbers of family and friends; include your own numbers and be aware that mobiles do not always work abroad. Other pages are for travel details and spare pages are for making notes, tearing out for messages and exchanging addresses with interesting people you meet.

Take the initiative, 'What's your address? I'll send you a Christmas card.' Also useful are those tiny stick on labels with your name and address.

Order low-denomination notes with your foreign currency and as soon as possible get some small change for tipping the kind man at the hotel who carries your luggage up and shows you how to work the lock in your room. Take a purse for storing UK money while you're abroad. Most hotels now have a safe in the wardrobe; use the same code number as your debit card pin number. In your pocket carry a small piece of card listing exchange rates for £1, £5, £10, and £100, saving the trouble of working it out each time.

Traditionally travellers were shown their room and if it was acceptable it formed a contract between you and the hotel. These days, particularly with a group, you are merely given a room number and key. Sit on the bed for a minute or two and look round. Single rooms are often rather small but if it is not right for you or if there is something you dislike tell reception before you unpack. In one hotel I was shown a tiny top floor room with a window so high I could only see through it by standing on a chair. Still wearing my coat I took the key down to reception and quietly asked to speak to the manager. 'Please can you find me another room,' I asked with a smile, 'I will pay extra if necessary.' I was given a spacious double room lower down in the hotel. It's best not to unpack too soon anyway because the brain stops working when you first arrive and you might forget where you put things. Keep your undies together in a bag inside the drawer. To know what to wear look through the window to see how the locals are dressed and if you want to look distinguished wear a big sunhat.

Be aware that if you speak a few words of a foreign language people think you know the whole of it and you could get in a mess.

Concentrate when it's time to leave because there's no husband to remind you to look behind the bathroom door. Once it's empty, tie a tissue round the handle of the wardrobe to save checking fifty times. On my first holiday alone I rang the hotel to say I'd left a pashmina behind. When the parcel came it contained, as well as the pashmina, a pair of walking socks, a nightdress, a library book and a camera. I'd left all that behind. Like a friend said, you're in a trance for the first year.

Pay for any extras on your hotel bill the night before you leave to save trouble on the last morning. In any case it's better to pay as you go because it's hard to remember what you ordered.

On adventurous long-haul flights try for a seat near the front of the plane where the air is better and for more legroom ask for an exit row. Thinking yourself into a new time zone helps with jetlag and travelling east is worse than west. About a week before, wear an extra watch set at the hour of your resort and continually be aware of the different times. Rethink the hours of daylight. Go to bed earlier and wake earlier. When you arrive at your destination you need to adjust as quickly as possible. Make no special plans for the first day and no matter how tired you are stay awake by drinking coffee and looking at the sunlight. If you wake too early stay in bed; by the third day your body clock will have adjusted.

Wife: *'I don't know why people make a fuss about jetlag. I never get it.'*

Husband: *'Well, why are you ironing at three o'clock in the morning?'*

Wife: *'I'm just not tired that's all.'*

P.S. Airlines are far more likely to upgrade the smart, single older lady than a couple.

Austrian Diary

I did not know what a chair-lift was as we set off that sunny morning with our guide. I did not know it was a metal airborne seat for one, with a single bar across, a seat I had to jump into while it was moving. I was terror-stricken and too timid to say so. Here's where the pose ends, here's where Mrs Superwoman changes into Mrs Frightened-to-Death. One by one the man thrusts my companions into their seats, snaps the bars down and launches them, feet dangling, into the air. Within seconds it's my turn. If they can do it I can do it and if I die, I die.

Not far below a man is scything grass with a rhythmic swing of his arm, so close I can hear him talking to his dog. The sweet, fresh scent of the cut grass fills the air; a meadow lush with purple clover, buttercups and other wild flowers all standing tall amidst plants and grasses of every shade of green. From where I sit, gently drifting upwards, a woman taking breakfast on her wooden balcony looks tilted. An orange cat pushes its way through the sward. A distant cowbell echoes. From an apple tree a blackbird pours its blessing into this bizarre silence and profound stillness. Alone with myself I am part of this amazing scene in my first year of widowhood. I had thought I had experienced every lovely thing and here I am, smoothly gliding. I love it. I am brave. I am a merry widow.

Now the passing scene changes into ranks of fir trees with darkness in between and the air becomes sharper and cold but I dare not relax my grip to adjust the coat our guide told us to wear.

Up ahead stand the mountain peaks, snow-covered and glistening against the startling blue of the sky like a painted stage set.

CRUISING

Going on a cruise is a wonderful idea. I've never actually been on a cruise myself but I sometimes like to imagine it.

You take all your best evening clothes, lacy with three-quarter sleeves, and hope you will be invited to the captain's table. Your berth will perhaps be rather small unless you've recently won the lottery or unearthed a cache of gold Roman coins in your garden. Wear a different flower in your hair every evening. You don't need to travel with a friend; cruise lines welcome single ladies, but of course if you have a congenial friend to go with who's also recently won the lottery or found treasure in her garden, that can be fun too.

Every day you disembark at a different harbour but remember to remove the flower in your hair from last night. Before leaving the ship, liner or boat take a good look round so you can remember which is yours when you come back among all the others when you come back, or you could take a photo of it or pin a label on your dress with the name of your ship on it. It must be awful to forget which liner or boat is yours.

Remember to change the time on your watch to local time. A friend who went on a cruise once returned to her ship to find it wasn't there. Remember to buy postcards of the vessel so you remember what it looks like when you've left it to go on a shore excursion.

Cruises are famous for, among other things, helping people to meet one another. Cruise lines are very conscious of the need for single ladies not to feel alone and they even provide dance partners, respectable members of the crew who are very good at dancing, to come along and dance with them.

The main thing about a cruise is that you have complete security, at least when you're on the ship anyway. Your possessions are all safe in your cabin and every morning, or every other morning depending on what the destination is, you wake up and find a wonderful new place to visit. It's a bit like being in a hotel in reverse. In a hotel you stay in one place and you have to move around; in a cruise it's the opposite. Also, depending on your budget, cruise holidays can be wonderfully luxurious. They're a kind of anticipation of heaven. You have a room or a suite which will be fitted out luxuriously. Normally it's the case that all meals are included. Additionally nowadays, because cruise operators realise that many elderly people get worried about tipping staff, what normally happens now is that tips are regarded as included and the cruise company simply pays the staff tips after the cruise has taken place. In fact, even though that's the case, I know that many people who go on cruises like to give their preferred staff a bit of extra money.

Of course, cruising can be a great way to meet a new husband and so not to be a merry widow any more but a merry wife!

If I did go on a cruise I think I'd like to go around the Mediterranean. It's the best place there is, isn't it really. It's the cradle of civilisation.

Cruise operators are very conscious that the ships themselves are a major attraction for customers and in fact cruise ships today are so wonderfully fitted out with amenities that many passengers don't bother going ashore at all. You've got any number of restaurants, you've got theatres, you got shooting ranges, if you fancy you can play tennis, you can even have a putting course. On one particular cruise liner nowadays there is a even an aerial overhead ride, you can have a climbing wall, though a merry widow's climbing days are probably over, if not necessarily forgotten. A journalist recently asked a public relations man working for a major cruise line:

'With all those amenities on the ship, is there actually any need to *go* anywhere at all?'

THE PLUMBER VISITS

Me   *'What shall I do about the water if I go away?'*

Plumber *'I've seen the damage burst pipes can do. Turn it off.'*

Me   *'Can you tell me how to do it?'*

Plumber *'Where's your stopcock?'*

Me   *'Down here. Help me pull the stove forward.'*

Plumber *'Sorry, I'm not allowed to move the stove. Health and Safety.'*

Me   *'Well I can't move it.'*

Plumber *'I could convert the stopcock to a simple wall switch.'*

Me   *'How much?'*

Plumber *'Ninety pounds.'*

Me   *'O.K. but what about moving the stove?'*

Plumber *'I'll do that for you.'*

Anniversary

My bridegroom gave me roses
All those years ago,
With flashing eyes and raven hair
He said he loved me so.

Trudging through the snow now
An old man you will see
But in his hands he's bringing
Red roses home for me.

Mary Essinger

12.
SOMEONE FOR THE WEEKEND MADAM?

My father used to say, 'Superior people do not make long visits.'

Marianne Moore

Guests must be chosen as carefully as the wine.

Saki

Answer these questions.

In your spare bedroom is the window more or less opaque?

Will fairy dust appear if you shake the curtain?

Do clothes spill out when you open the wardrobe?

Are you amazed at the number of suitcases that can be stored under a bed?

And rolls of wallpaper?

Does the waste-paper basket still conceal a make up stain on the carpet?

Does the newspaper lining the drawer date from the last century?

Or even the one before that?

If your answers are mostly 'yes' you are becoming a spare room slut and in danger of excommunication by the Merry Widow Society. Take urgent action. Invite a friend for the weekend and spend an exciting time transforming the room into five-star luxury accommodation for one.

Even if you're terrific at decorating don't do it yourself, get a professional in; merry widows do not spend three days splattered with emulsion paint. Choose any colour except beige and, as part of the deal, see that he takes his rubbish away. Allow at least three weeks for the paint smell to disappear.

New walls need a new carpet, take the measurements with you but have them checked by the fitter before ordering. Keep to one plain colour, not beige, and as part of this deal, get him to take the old carpet away.

If you are washing lined curtains turn them inside out, keeping the hooks in, and hang them up before they are completely dry to let the creases drop out. There's a lot of work to do but the best part is to come.

Arrange the room beautifully. Except for books remove all your own ornaments and bric a brac, leaving one modern picture on the wall. Empty the wardrobe apart from a bathrobe and towelling slippers all freshly washed, together with twelve matching hangers, some with lavender bags tied on with mauve ribbon. There's no need to empty all the drawers but spread sheets of tissue paper over their contents. On the bed place two towels, one big, one small, not beige, tied round with ribbon for a feminine touch and a dainty bar of soap on top. In winter, leave an extra blanket and a hot-water bottle.

As well as a table to put things on, a chair to sit in and a stand for luggage, your visitor will need a reading light near the bed, a radio in case she can't sleep and some organic chocolate to nibble while she's tuned in to the World

Service at three o'clock in the morning and you wake up thinking it's a burglar.

As a treat for both of you, book a theatre visit and, as well as a freezer full of your superb home cooking, plan at least one meal out. Look forward to the weekend yourself; after living alone you will once again have the pleasure of saying to someone, 'Come on, we're going out.'

Finish all preparations the day before she arrives; as long as the bathroom and kitchen are clean the rest doesn't matter. So what if everything isn't perfect? She's coming to see you, not the house and if you overdo things it might put her off inviting you back. Remember the best is yet to come.

Your guest will be tired after her journey, greet her with a cup of tea before showing her the amazing room. Tell her to treat the house as her own and to use anything in the bathroom, which she probably would anyway. Leave her to unpack and do not enter her room again; this is her personal space.

Ignore all these instructions if your guest is male because they arrive late, plonk their open case in the middle of the floor, spend every hour on your computer and gobble up everything in the fridge. Unless of course he's gay in which case he'll tell you what to do and he'll iron the curtains for you as well.

Breakfast is tricky, good guests stay in their room till they're called down. Take the initiative by saying, 'Bacon and eggs will be ready at nine, is that OK?' with luck she'll only want toast and coffee. If she offers to help in the kitchen give her the pretty apron and gloves you've so thoughtfully provided.

Your visitor does not need to be constantly entertained. Don't fuss, if she sees you quietly reading she will do the same and if she needs anything she'll say so. You could ask if there's a favourite TV programme she would be sorry to miss.

Now for the best part. This comes when she leaves and you're on your own again. Alone to talk to yourself, change into comfy trousers, leave the dishes till morning, swear a bit, eat delicious leftovers, drink coffee from a mug in front of TV, phone a friend, stay up late and on the way to bed admire your beautiful spare room.

True friendship's laws are by this rule expressed
Welcome the coming, speed the parting guest.

Alexander Pope

13.
MOVING ON

You need to be on a bus route, near shops, near a library and near a doctor.

Social worker

When merry widows get together they often talk about going to live somewhere else but they all agree that moving too soon is not a good idea because you lose your home as well as your husband. Some widows sell up and move to another part of the country where they don't know anybody. To be near her daughter one moved to Norwich and a year later the daughter moved to Australia. Perhaps it was something mother said.

Friend - I used to run a hotel in Cornwall. Lots of retired people moved there.
Fifty per cent of them regretted it.

Look what older people leave behind if they move to a new area; a whole network of friends and acquaintances that's taken years to build up. One of the first things people say when they meet someone new is, 'Oh, you live there? Do you know so and so?' and off they go finding connections. We go to a certain café knowing we may well run into a friend, even if it's just a wave across the tables. Imagine going round the shops in a strange town and not seeing one familiar face. Not one person who might wave across the street. Why give all that up? And look at the other familiar network of plumbers, electricians, hairdressers, health services; who wants to start from scratch with all that again?

Health is a major factor in deciding the ideal accommodation for merry widows. New research indicates that with modern medicines most women between seventy and eighty enjoy comparatively good health and it's not until they reach eighty that they start to become frail.

A widow aged ninety-five - *If you are going to move don't leave it till you are too old. Do it while you are in good health.*

A big house takes a lot of cleaning and you're forever going up and down stairs trying to remember whether you left the car keys in the bedroom or indeed where the bedroom is. Houses cost a lot to heat but when I asked a bridge friend why widows don't live together she said it was because they couldn't stand the sight of each other! Another way of dealing with the expense of a big house is to take in lodgers but you need to be extremely tolerant of different kinds of people occupying your space and tolerant of your neighbours' jokes and whisperings. A friend lets rooms to actors from the local theatre, enjoying their company immensely (and the free tickets) but they have their own bathroom and kitchen and live separately.

Merry widows love bungalows because there are no stairs and you don't need a window-cleaner because you can reach all the windows yourself if you stand on tiptoe. What you can't do is leave windows open in summer in case somebody comes in and pinches your pension and all the neighbours will be bus-pass people talking about their tablets. Another problem is that your knees stop working because they've forgotten how to climb up steps and you have go out every day to find some to practise on.

A widow speaks - *I'm selling my bungalow to move into a rented apartment because I don't want to spend money and time on property repairs. I want to be free to enjoy myself while I can.*

A widow speaks - *Whatever you do, don't live in a cul de sac; you need to be where you can see people passing by.*

A widow speaks - *This house cost much less than the bungalow I sold and as well as making money I love it here. I could spend hours just looking out of the upstairs windows and seeing all the gardens; you can't do that in a bungalow. I could always get a stair-lift if I needed one.*

A stair-lift that is, not a chair-lift. There's a big difference... An apartment has no garden but there might be a balcony where you can grow red geraniums in terracotta pots. If you enjoy weeding and the smell of newly-cut grass don't even think about moving to an apartment.

First you buy the apartment then you pay something called a service charge to cover property maintenance and this figure goes up from time to time. You won't feel isolated because there will be a lot of people around, which is OK if they are your sort of people.

Some apartments have special entrance gates for security and when your friends visit they must leave their car in the street, approach the gate and key in your number (if they can remember it) then wait in the rain till you open the gate by remote control (if you know how to do it.) At last they come in but I have no idea how they get out again, or indeed whether they ever do.

A widow speaks - *My parents moved into an apartment when they were both in their eighties and immediately regretted it because they felt cut off from other people. They used to enjoy a ten-minute walk to the shops every day but their first outing from the apartment was a long uphill drag and when they came back they were almost on their knees. My father became ill on the third day and by the end of the week he was dead.*

Mother moved to a retirement village of bungalows with a community lounge and lots of social activities. She is very happy there.

A widow speaks - *In this apartment we are all widows and we help each other. If we haven't seen anybody for a day or two we knock on the door. It's wonderful but I wouldn't choose the ground floor for security reasons; I think I've read too many thrillers.*

Dotted round the country are pretty developments called retirement villages with trees and water features and an assortment of bungalows and houses all among flowers and birdsong.

The rooms in these dwellings are rather small because it is assumed that older people will be sitting still all the time. There is some kind of warden and lots of socialising and outings. People certainly seemed happy there when I drove to see a friend but she told me I was too young and nowhere near ready even to contemplate joining her. It was worth the visit to be told that. She also said the active residents were constantly being asked by others to do little jobs like carrying shopping from the car or collecting a prescription.

The very thought of sorting out a lifetime's possessions and transferring them to another address is terrifying. After all, moving can be stressful even if you really like the place you are going to. You could think about disposing of surplus furniture now in case you decide to move somewhere smaller. Unless it has antique value furniture is hard to sell and even harder to give away. Voluntary organisations will not accept upholstered furniture without a fire certificate; you'd be amazed at the beautiful three-piece suites looking unloved at council refuse tips.

There is of course always the option of staying put and embracing inertia until you become so ancient and decrepit that somebody has to carry you away to a nursing home in a Rolls Royce.

RETIREMENT COMMUNITIES

Since writing this book - which was first published in 2007, though I've revised it since then and added some additional material eg. this bit - I've moved into a retirement apartment community in a lovely community in a nice part of Leicester.

My husband and I were always wondering about moving to live somewhere new once the children had left home, but we stayed in the modern detached house we bought in 1975.

Once, visiting a posh area of Leicester, we admired some newly-built apartments and coming through the side gate was a friend I knew by sight and I asked her if she liked living there. 'It's wonderful,' she said. 'The trouble is that if you come to live here you need to accept that it means you're getting old.'

My dear husband Ted passed away in 2005, and we hadn't moved. But in 2015 I took the plunge and went to live in one of those retirement apartments in that very place where Ted and I had taken a look.

I recall the pleasure of moving day, once all the furniture was delivered, and I made tea for the men and bought sandwich packs. My eldest son and his friend Francesca helped them.

After Ted's death, at first it was very strange living alone. But friends used to say to me, 'if you are thinking of leaving don't hang on, just do it because the longer you wait the less likely you are to do it and the younger you are you've got the energy to do it, so don't think that you can just do it all when you are eighty, because you can't.'

It got to the point where I used to lie in bed alone at night in the house and hear noises and things and it got to the point that that was how I went to sleep every night listening intently to see if there was anybody trying to break in.

Simply put, there came a point in my life where I wasn't really that comfortable in the house any more. It was too big for me and I wasn't quite as mobile as I was before. I'd abandoned driving some years ago for example.

This is a lovely area called Stoneygate in Leicester and all those beautiful, posh houses and these apartments – I think there used to be a police station there, that's what people have told me. It used to be a police station and now there are these apartments.

These retirement communities should not to be confused with nursing homes. Retirement communities really are communities, where elderly people can live very much their own lives. They can see their friends here when they want to and they can have time to themselves when they want that.

We have a super communal room and I love the profusion of flowers and the way the buildings are designed. My eldest son says affectionately that the buildings remind him of some of the buildings in the Shire – the hobbits' homeland in *Lord of the Rings* - and I really felt it was a home from home and it came to me without any of the downsides of having my own house and not feeling that secure. That's a major advantage of living in a house or apartments in a retirement community: you feel secure and safe. Lots of times you go on holiday, even if we want to leave the apartment you just want to think oh well, perhaps somebody could break in...

Another great advantage for me of living in this kind of community is that I feel much safer when I go on holiday, I don't feel the house is likely to get broken into because I know it's all very secure and there aren't too many stairs and there is quite a bit of social life. It's true that sometimes I wish there was more communal activity but in fact we do have quite a lot of it, such as a Scrabble night, a fish and chip night, talks, trips, communal meals and so on. One of my favourite meals there is Lancashire hotpot. We all have to book it of course and then they pick up the washing up from outside. They're lovely these communal meals.

Another thing I want to say is that people often imagine retirement communities are full of doddery elderly folk. There are a few of those about here it's true, but many of the people who live here are actually retired professionals, for example one of my gentlemen neighbours is a former police chief inspector who simply finds this a very good way of living and in fact some people live here and are continuing to work because the minimum age in my particular retirement community is fifty-five, so people can be living here and working and it is a convenient place for them to live. In fact my eldest son is old enough to live here if he wanted to!

I found that living in a retirement community was a new start for me, a new life. Both my sons come and visit me and they have a new lease of life with me here as well, it's a new life for us all.

Acknowledgements

SPECIAL THANKS TO:
  Lydia, Brenda, Anne T, Ann, Eileen, Audrey, Peggy,
  June D, Pat, Francis, Glennis, Janet, Margaret, Steve,
  Gloria, Jean, Gillian, Gill, Colin, Peter, Pam and Mavis.
  Jack, Gerta
  Members of Leicester Writers' Club
  Simon Hoggart
  My thanks to Dianne Norton of the Third Age Press
for agreeing to the reprint of this revised edition of this
book. Full details of all Third Age Press publications can
be found on www.thirdagepress.co.uk
  My thanks also to Charlotte Mouncey for the superb
cover and typesetting and to James Essinger my publisher
at The Conrad Press.